ON CHINA AND CUBA

ON CHINA AND CUBA

by

José M. Gironella

Translated, with a prologue, by
JOHN F. BYRNE

FIDES PUBLISHERS, INC.
NOTRE DAME, INDIANA

Library of Congress Catalog Card Number: 63-20806

The China part of this book appeared originally in the Spanish periodical *Gaceta illustrada,* under the title "Viaje en torno a la revolución china." The Cuba part of this book was published in *Todos Somos Fugitvos* (Editorial Planeta, Barcelona) under the title "Viaje en torno a la revolución cubana."

Manufactured by North State Press, Inc., Hammond, Indiana

TRANSLATOR'S PROLOGUE

The fascinating questions raised by international Communism's relentless advance across large areas of Europe and Asia, and its more recent beachhead in Latin America, have challenged a number of modern writers. The tone of their studies has ranged from alarm to ecstatic praise, with a generous sampling of disillusioned former Communists setting forth their bitter sense of betrayal. Current trends in the Communist world, including the phenomenon of the first serious threat to the Soviet Union's primacy since the 1917 Revolution, have focused attention on China and Cuba. The prospect of China's development of nuclear weapons and Cuba's transformation into the Western Hemisphere's first full-fledged Communist state have created new shifts in the global balance of power whose consequences we are just beginning to experience.

The subjects of these two essays are unique among José Maria Gironella's writings and not typical of his work; it is for this reason that he has asked me to try to explain the motives behind his choice of subject. Gironella himself needs no introduction to the American public. His extraordinary novel, *The Cypresses Believe in God*, which won the Thomas More Award in the U.S., aroused great

v

24785

interest and expectation for the second part of the trilogy, *One Million Dead* (Doubleday, 1963). His reputation as a novelist, essayist, journalist and humanist is firmly secure in Europe, where the two sections of his trilogy on post-monarchy Spain published to date have established him as one of the really authoritative voices of a modern Spain whose Second Republic was betrayed by the far Left and given the final coup de grace by the far Right.

Gironella's preoccupation with Communism as a socio-historical phenomenon is due to the violent eruption it has caused in contemporary history; his deeper preoccupation is related to the fact that its enormous vigor and the apostolic zeal of its disciples have stolen the role of moral and social pacesetter which once corresponded to Christianity. Gironella has told me that he prophesies the vertical collapse of Communism as such, as a doctrine. Meanwhile, however, the potential consequences of the system makes one's blood run cold.

His vivid interest in China and Cuba, individually and in juxtaposition, stems from the fact that one is the heir to an old, European-Christian tradition and saturated in Occidental culture, whereas the other is an ancient nation with an ethical, cultural and religious code all its own. They represent the two extremes of the world-wide Communist experiment. Cuba is the smallest nation to serve as the stage for the Marxist rehearsal and China is the largest nation. This highlights a type of dualism and, at the same time, a contrast which could be most instructive. The dualism is based upon the similarity between Mao and Fidel, each in his own fief, and the apparent and (in Gironella's opinion) deepening failure of Communism in both countries. The contrast lies in their distinct relationships to the U.S.S.R. Fidel still depends almost entirely upon the Soviet Union, while Mao is becoming progressively more independent, although perhaps not quite so much as the West thinks, and is likely to possess his own nuclear bomb.

The idea for these two studies lay in Gironella's mind for some time. He visited Cuba briefly in the summer of 1961, after an extensive study of the Castro Revolution. His conclusions cannot help but be tempered by the instinctive reflections of a Spaniard for whom Cuba is a former part of a once-great empire, still linked intimately to the Motherland by ties of language, religion and culture. Even today, apart from commercial considerations, it is undoubtedly nostalgia, a sentimental sense of loyalty which accounts for Spain's continued maintenance of diplomatic relations with Cuba. Spanish shipping and air lines are among Cuba's few remaining links with the West and as such one of the main routes of escape for refugees. As Gironella says, the ships of the Spanish Transatlantic Line seem to navigate the course to the Caribbean all by themselves after so many years.

His observations on China are not the result of any personal visit to the country but rather of a penetrating research. The Orient has attracted him for some time. He recently returned from an extended trip through Japan with his intimate friend, the classical guitarist, Narciso Yepes, and was intrigued by this contact with a non-Christian culture, just as he was on a previous trip to the Middle East. I recall a memorable few hours we spent at a sidewalk cafe in Barcelona one sunny Spring afternoon last year. We rambled on through a provocative series of "what ifs": what would have happened if Spain had not expelled the Jews in the fifteenth century, if she had not sent forth so many thousands of her young men to conquer and colonize America, if José Antonio Primo de Rivera had not been killed? One of the most absorbing questions regarded what might have happened to Christianity in the Far East if its early missionaries had not been forced to conform to a rigidly Occidental approach: might the Orient conceivably be Christian today?

How responsible are Batista and Chiang Kai-shek for what is happening today in Cuba and China? To what extent have Capitalism's social errors prepared the way and made a Communist takeover possible? How great a threat to the world's peace and security do these two nations pose? There is an endless series of disturbing questions for the thoughtful reader in these essays of Gironella. Translating them was as enjoyable as it was simple. The great charm of his style is what one critic has termed his ". . . austere, grey prose, shot through with rare, unexpected shafts of brilliant sunlight." The very personal pleasure and honor this translation represents for me is matched only by that of the author's friendship.

John F. Byrne
Madrid, 1963

CONTENTS

CHINA

CUBA

CHINA

1

WIND FROM THE EAST

One day while Confucius was resting he was approached by four of his disciples, Tse-lun, Kung-si Hwa, Zan Yu and Tseng-hsi. The Wise One spoke to them individually, questioning them about their ambitions. The first told him that he wished to build a strong and powerful nation. The second said that his ambition was to be sufficiently clever and capable to bring prosperity to the people. The third declared that his dream was to direct the protocol and ceremonies of the state as nobody had ever done. The fourth disciple, Tseng-hsi, declined to reply and went on playing his lyre. At length, in view of the Master's insistence, he answered: "My desire is quite different. When spring comes, I wish to go with my friends to bathe in the River Yi, enjoying the lovely shade and the freshness of the Altar of Rain and, afterwards, return home singing."

It was Tseng-hsi who received Confucius' blessing.

Old Chinese Legend

This brief Confucian tale might well illustrate the biography of China's current leader, Mao Tse-tung, the father of the Chinese Communist revolution. In fact, in his speeches as well as his books, books which are presently studied in all the Chinese universities, Mao Tse-tung has expressed the triple wish of the first three of Confucius' disciples: to establish a strong, powerful state, to be clever and capable enough to enrich his country, and to direct the ceremonies and protocol of the nation. It is Tseng-hsi whom Mao has yet to imitate; for that, the Chinese ruler would have to concentrate on playing the lyre, bathing in the river and returning home singing with his friends. Instead, Mao prefers to build smelting furnaces and gigantic dams, to dry swamps and plan highways. Instead, he prefers to build prisons for his enemies and hear millions of Chinese chanting in unison:

> Union creates strength,
> A strength made of iron,
> A strength made of steel.

Two months before his death, Nikos Kazantzakis, the famous Greek writer, author of *The Greek Passion* and other novels, announced that he wished to visit Peking once more. He said:

We of the West haven't the vaguest idea of what China's intrinsic strength is. We judge China as if she had only been in existence for a hundred years—precisely these past hundred years in which the country has lived in a state of semi-colonial decadence. We forget that China's area is slightly greater than Canada's and that for five thousand years China's military glory carried her warriors far beyond her borders, from Mongolia and Korea to Indochina and Turkestan. We forget that she conquered the great plains of eastern Asia for her agriculture, that she opened the silk route to Persia and India, and established her naval pre-eminence as far as the Indian Ocean. China has been dozing, napping for a century, because the laws of nature require that even dragons have to rest sometime. But she has never stopped dreaming of expansion, of pouring over all of Asia and Europe, just as within her borders the Hwang Ho and the Yangtze overflow their banks. In my opinion, the moment for her to wake up and stretch has come. People were mistaken when they thought that the current revolution, begun in 1949 with the rise to power of the Communist Party, was an exclusively economic revolution. It is something more: it is a messianic revolution. Its supporters aren't merely boasting when they claim that "the East Wind is blowing more strongly now than the West Wind." Mao Tse-tung—politician, soldier, thinker and poet—proposes to turn his ancestors' dreams of conquest into reality.

The testimonies supporting this opinion of Kazantzakis's are abundant. There is hardly an international observer who hasn't felt a sudden, involuntary chill upon looking at a map of China. What will happen when the country is industrialized? Who will control the dragon once the 4,500 geological teams sent to Sinkiang, Tibet, and the mountainous regions in the southwest locate the immense natural wealth buried there? China knows how to smile sweetly but her smile is far from being a good-natured grin. The Chinese are guided by a concept of good and evil very different from ours. They have never believed that God created man to His image and likeness; perhaps it is for this reason that they concede to human life a much less sacred value than in the West.

Latest figures put the current number of Chinese at over 650 million, or in other words, a quarter of humanity. One out of every four inhabitants of the earth is Chinese.

To my way of thinking, those 650 million people constitute the perfect arsenal for the world-wide Asiatic domination which many observers forsee. Mao Tse-tung never misses an opportunity to refer to this human avalanche, which is more than triple the Slavic population. The Chinese leader has interpreted this fact as a good omen: "Our hour has arrived."

The consistent reply of the West has been: "Bah! So much has been said about the oriental masses! What difference do masses make? The whites will continue to stay on top." But this is the nervous answer of people bent on survival. The Chaldeans and the ancient Egyptians must have made similar statements when the world was making ready to swallow them up, reducing their civilizations to a few sarcophagi and some astrological tables. The white race has always thought this way because of its belief in the triumph of intelligence and because, for centuries, it has always been able to dominate distant masses with crossbows or rifles. This is a strong argument, and, after all, hasn't it always been valid until now? And yet, will it continue to be valid from now on? May not a radical change have taken place, as the result of a logical evolution? Are the Chinese masses still as amorphous as in the days of the philosopher Mencius?

These are questions without answers. It is clear that there is a practically unchangeable sentiment deep within the soul of every primitive people; stirring it up is a colossal task. The people lack the necessary intellectual flexibility, and yet—we need only look around to see what is happening. Just as the Arabs are claiming their rights, urged on by fanatical but impeccably dressed leaders who studied at the Sorbonne, just as India has preserved her rituals but is beginning to break down the barriers of caste and is eagerly being treated with vaccines made in the West, and just as democratic customs have penetrated the Japanese imperial palace, so too China is mechanizing and industrializing. These terms—"mechanize" and "industrialize"—are tremendously important and completely change the whole picture. Once the mechanization and industrialization are completed, then population statistics will indeed count, and the fantastic potential manpower of China will take on new significance. Six hundred and fifty million workers using machines are not the same as 650 million condemned to a lifetime of agonizing manual labor.

And furthermore, this huge mass now has a powerful leader, Mao Tse-tung, whose authority serves as an adhesive to prevent dispersion and softness. It has been said that Mao's power is comparable to that of the ancient emperors whom the Chinese venerated as "agents" of the gods; it is probably far greater, since it is an *active* power which is more and more efficient as time goes by and is not content with a merely flattering obedience, traditional and tending toward lethargy. Instead, this power is attempting to turn China into the most industrious beehive in the world's history. In addition, Mao's authority is greater than Lenin's or even Stalin's since it is exercised over a people infinitely more accustomed to continuous slavery and misery.

This is certainly another of the several realities of present-day China which are changing the rules of the game; China has been familiar with wretchedness for centuries and consequently is likely to accept more or less calmly any sacrifice asked of her. China is the martyr-nation par excellence. It would be difficult to find on the map any civilized area so cut off from security. Natural catastrophes, floods, famines and plagues—all have ravaged the Celestial Empire's extensive territories again and again, crushing them much the same way one crushes a coffee bean underfoot. The Chinese farmer's complexion is the color of the earth and when he speaks, displaying his variable phonetics, he seems to be lamenting his ill fortune.

China's misery has always been relentless. The words "misery" and "hunger" have a very concrete meaning in

China which is difficult for an Occidental to grasp. "When it blows, three feet of dust; when it rains, the street is no more than mud," says an old Chinese expression. In China the rivers are not *in* the plains but *on* the plains. In periods of drought or flood the farmers do not say "hello" when they meet, but rather: "Have you eaten today?"

In China it has always been common to see women and children carrying on their backs over long distances the water needed to irrigate a plot of land the size of a handkerchief. On all sides there are huts of clay and bamboo. On all sides, the pitiful farmers, kneeling or up to their ankles in water. In the south, they eat a little rice; in the north, a little wheat or millet. Most of them are sick with beriberi, pellagra, and illnesses of fecal origin, caused by the human excrement so commonly used as fertilizer. Many of these peasants lack even a name of their own, having instead nicknames inspired by their physical deformities: Broken-nose, Cut-ear, Short-leg, etc. They are a deeply superstitious people, subject to primitive fears and forebodings which are usually connected with the more extravagant phenomena of nature. Periodically, such peasants decide to relocate, to emigrate, with a small bundle on their backs as their only wealth. Before leaving they beg pardon of their ancestors' spirits for abandoning their tombs. They are an ingenuous people, obstinate and rather inclined toward games of chance; occasionally they have their moments of humor—strange to say, while watering the fields. Their principal social unit is the family, a rock-bound clan under the strict authority of the male head. There have been families which, according to the circumstances and driven on by hunger, have done away with newborn children or amputated their limbs so that later on they might cause greater compassion when they began begging. There are families that have known cannibalism, or have risked death for a trifle, a fan or a cup of tea.

The enormous misery of China defies all description and constitutes one of the capital sins of historic man, if we consider him responsible for what happens in a distant orchard on a distant desert. Whatever the circumstances of the present seismic movement underway in China, the West—a disinterested if not a downright usurious bystander —has probably deserved them.

Intimately familiar with his people's idiosyncrasies, Mao Tse-tung began right from the first moment of his revolutionary adventure to speak directly to his subjects about the possibility of improving their lot, a possibility now offered them for the first time in history, by the Communist Party. Communism was the most beautiful creation of modern times, he assured them, able in itself to change all the patterns of routine and monotony. It was a global view of life created, in Russia to be exact, by men who had likewise suffered hunger and persecution and it had taken into account all the contingencies which might crop up in a society. Specially oriented as it was toward underdeveloped countries with immense unexploited natural resources, toward "peoples abandoned by the mythical God and by man's greediness," Communism seemed made to order for the redemption of China. It was not merely another theory which got lost in the air like a kite or the words of a charla⸱ tan; no, it was a new Tablet of the Laws which was concrete for a change and faced problems head-on. When he addressed himself to the 500 million peasants intent on his manner and gestures, Mao raised his hand in a closed-fist salute, waved his short-brimmed cap—a Longchamp jockey's cap—and assured his audience that although the Chinese Communist Party was growing, it still had only three million members; this was due to the same ignorance which had always plagued the nation and which even now kept him from finding the anchor of salvation. "We have been as ignorant as our farmers, who, having the ocean nearby, nonetheless complain about the lack of water for the crops."

Mao announced the Communist Party's program and at the same time indicated what the Party expected of the people:

To prevent floods, the Party will construct with your help a series of dikes over ninety feet high. It will dry the swamps and make it possible to farm them. It will build highways and railroads to link the rich provinces with the poor ones. In the event of a catastrophe there will always be a little rice or a little wheat left in the bottoms of your cups so that you can survive until the next harvest. In return, I ask for your help, since a fire burns better if everyone contributes his piece of wood. We shall build a great green wall to the north of the Gobi Desert; millions of trees will be planted to break the deadly cold wind which sweeps down from Siberia. Until now the West has exploited us, treating us with disdain as though we were puppets like we have in our theatres. But "Communism is good," as our song says, and will free us. When Communism has triumphed, the sun of justice in the Celestial Empire will shine for everyone.

This terminology was new and smelled of fresh bread and resurrection. The Chinese people were excited and side by side in a display of solidarity they shouted: "Ten thousand years of life to Mao!" Mao's catchwords spread across the ancient map of China, engulfing it just as one's soul is sometimes overwhelmed by a warm emotion. Mao saw his call answered to overflowing. Engel's slogan, "War on the palaces, peace in the huts," was repeated to any who wavered. Under Mao's leadership the Communist Party grew rapidly, almost unbelievably. The balloon of complacency burst, startling Chiang Kai-shek, Mao's inveterate rival. Generalissimo Chiang Kai-shek, "firmly set in the ways of the old system," was labeled a "reactionary" and "imperialist." His troops moved against Mao and forced him to flee to the mountains, which only served to intensify the brilliance of his halo. It was inevitable that Mao would win out at last, as he finally did in the year 1949. "The sun of justice" began to shine, although not on everyone, while in Peking the bells of the Kremlin could be heard.

Once victory had been achieved, its contagion followed and soon spread everywhere. The Chinese people swarmed en masse to the Summer Palace in Peking, one of the residences selected by Mao, and shouted ceaselessly: "Ten thousand years' of life to Mao!" Then Mao, determined to start his people along the path to greatness, informed them that according to the astrologists, both China and the United States were under the same sign, that of Cancer ruled by the moon. China ought therefore to imitate the United States in certain ·practical aspects, although not of course in its spiritual aspects. China, abandoned for centuries, now ought to take the "Great Leap Forward"; this expression became the official slogan, and nobody could reasonably oppose such a desire.

By all the means of communications at his disposal, Mao reviewed for his people the ancient privileges enjoyed by the nation's despotic exploiters. Over the radio he read the menus common at the banquets of the old dynasties and ridiculed the wealthy Chinese who let their fingernails grow long, protecting them with special metal covers, so that no one would think they had to perform manual labor. He denounced the administrative corruption of the final phase of the Chiang government—imagine, the nation's coffers in the hands of his in-laws, the Soongs!—and enumerated the fortunes piled up by the rich Chinese living abroad. He enjoyed tracing historical syntheses: "Our race, the Chinese race," he said, "has made invaluable contributions to mankind's progress. Aside from philosophy, unique in its profundity, China invented the first network of canals, the first armored car, the cultivation of silk worms, weaving, fermented rice, woodpulp and paper, the compass, the first printing press, the first engravings, gunpowder. . . . Paper was useful to our ancestors for transmitting their teachings from one generation to another. The compass oriented them in their search for a means of salvation, ineffective for so many centuries. And gunpowder will now be useful for our revolution, the socialist revolution."

The people responded. China was turned into one giant workshop, of dimensions never before seen by man. Millions of volunteers and millions of forced laborers, working at machine pace, contributed their pieces of wood so that, in Mao's words, the first might burn better. From Manchuria to the quarries of Wuchang, from the industrial region of Chungking to the endless wildernesses, along the roads and the rivers, all of them worked to build the modern China and awake from their semi-colonial lethargy. Persons retired because of old age took up their plows, pick-axes, or the classic coolie-pole with its two buckets and returned to work. Women gave up the "small individual home" and joined the "big socialized home." Many soldiers, upon being demobilized, asked to work for the Party rather than to return home. The working conditions of these jobs, inhuman for any Occidental, were accepted without complaint. What China had known up till then had been much worse, they reasoned. True, every new day saw more and more corpses in the ditches and on the river banks, but what was so unusual about that? Had not entire communities died without pity and without glory in years past? "Why it is," shouted Mao, "that the West now protests about the death of laborers on the dikes of the Yellow River when only recently it said nothing when the overflowing of that same river drowned hundreds? Those who die today die in order to save future lives." And Chou En-lai, Premier and executor of Mao's doctrine, observed: "Perhaps the West came to our aid in the past when it heard our cries? No, it pretended not to understand our language, Chinese." Yes, everyone agreed that at last China had a chance; China had hope. The eastern part of the country had always been fertile but the western part was rough and barren. There were too many camels and elephants and too few tractors. The hour of redemption had come. The famous Great Wall of China, three thousand miles long, had been built with slave labor. Why wasn't it possible to build, with everyone's help, first Socialism and then Communism? Chou En-lai continued to produce promising statistics and print tons of posters which represented China's enemies, the Western imperialists, in ridiculous situations, being chased by gigantic Chinese.

The West watched this course of events with a sudden and complex uneasiness. The general theory was that Marxism would run into invincible problems in China. Such theorists speculated about the characteristics considered basic in the Chinese personality, for example: respect for elders, the sense of family, the inclination toward private enterprise, and a dread of centralized government. How would such resistances be met and defeated? They were as opposed to orthodox Marxism as health is to sickness, and as the land is to the sea. The whole world began to consult the ouija board and drag out dusty old volumes of Confucius and Lao-tse in an attempt to find an answer.

Meanwhile, Mao—who incidentally continued to write the finest calligraphic hand in China, which earned him even greater respect—paid little attention to such abstractions and began to study future Five Year Plans. With this end in mind he was to submit his country to a terrific struggle passing all limits of endurance.

Mao, with the benevolent smile of a "Father of the Country," was brewing for China the greatest revolutionary tumult in history.

This tumult, with its inevitable ups and downs, has persisted to this day. What are the results? No one can honestly claim that Marxism, in its fourteen years in power, has triumphed in China; all the foreseen reflexes have cropped up and obliged Mao Tse-tung to backtrack in some cases, such as the People's Communes and the anti-conception campaign. But neither can it be claimed that the Communist Party's labors have been in vain. Mao has pushed through all of the legislation he wanted and, especially in the fields of industry and public works—the classic pivots of a dictatorship—has achieved advances which will become a permanent part of China. Mao's China, in spite of the nightmares of hunger and mortality, in spite of a natural longing for liberty and the incessant struggles with the Soviet Union, is still prepared to pull an ace or two out of her sleeve and surprise the world, and maybe dominate it. For this purpose Mao Tse-tung maintains an army out of all proportion to the nation's defense needs, hysterically demands the secret of atomic energy from the Kremlin, and regularly knocks at Hong Kong's door.

Will Mao succeed in burying the Old China, as he has promised? Will he manage to impose his new beliefs and his new loyalties on the people or, on the other hand, will the innermost spirit of the race absorb him as a frog swallows a mosquito? It is a novel, fascinating, and ruthless fight. Mao has decided to rule out affection and the imperatives of the heart, to an even greater degree than Soviet Russia. More than Russia itself, Mao has deified matter and the influence of economic and production factors. He has not run up against Christianity, as in Russia. His people are used to waiting. These tremendous questions remain unanswered, and in order to decipher and answer them in advance one would have to be God.

2

---◆---

MAO AND HIS RISE TO POWER

"Ten thousand years of life to Mao!" This cry echoes throughout forests and steppes all across China. Before, the Chinese soldier with his parasol was a laughing-stock all around the world; now, thanks to Mao, he inspires terror rather than humor. Years ago in the Manchu era, the Chinese wore braids—symbols of submission which one could tug to humiliate the wearer; the Chinaman's braid has now practically disappeared. In the cities, thanks to Mao, the carts and wagons are exchanging their antiquated wheels for rubber tires. In the country, landlords have been eliminated and the tractor has begun to put in its appearance. Prostitution has declined greatly, being replaced by "collective entertainments," many of which are christened with poetic names. China today, thanks again to Mao, is on the front pages across the world, much to the gloomy surprise of her Asian neighbors.

Mao is seventy years old. He was born into a family of prosperous farmers in 1893, the same year that Taine, de Maupassant, Gounod and Tchaikowsky died. His birth took place on December 26, the day after the celebration of Christ's birthday, at eight o'clock in the morning; his family lived in the region of Hunan, southern China. According to Chinese calculations he was thus born in the year of the Black Serpent, in the month of the Green Rat, on the day of the Red Rooster and at the hour of the Dragon.

His childhood and adolescence were spent in primary education, the normal schools of Hunan as well as private studies. The overwhelming revolutionary personality of Sun Yat-sen, "Father of the Chinese Revolution," the death of the old Empress Tzu Hsi and the fall of the Empire in 1911 awakened his political vocation, and he wrote his first article, which he promptly pasted up on the wall of his school; but his first great love was poetry, especially the Chinese and Persian classics. He enrolled early in the University of Peking in the modest capacity of assistant librarian, and found there plenty of material to satisfy his thirst for reading. The sense of filial loyalty present in all of Confucius' works acted as a brake on his development, which otherwise would have been more rapid in view of the empirical and despotic nature of Chinese family life. In addition, the uncompromising pacifism of Lao-tse somewhat slowed up his embryonic plans for reform at any cost. Nevertheless, he admired the great patriotic thinkers, recording their sayings in his mind: "The prince should not be over-estimated by the people, as some unique gem." "The superior man is the one who never loses control of his thoughts."

Mao wanted to become a superior man. His health was precarious, so everything would have to depend on his will power. There was one fact in his favor: the turn of the century, which terrorized innumerable people—prophets of doom had announced that the end of the world would occur in 1900—did not upset him in the least. It has been said that since his childhood Mao Tse-tung has seemed to consider himself above good and evil. Reserved in appearance, his cheeks fill out like apples when he smiles, and he seems fatter. His hands are broad and limber, peculiar to a man who gives blessings or one who perspires. Intelligence peers obliquely from his eyes, but none of his features is ascetic and when he walks it could almost be said that he waddles; at the same time, he appears to want to sink into the ground. He likes to analyse problems conscientiously and seek the truth beneath surface appearances. In the country, in the fields, he seems to confront reality free from encumbrances, naked and solitary; for this reason, he goes there frequently, to contemplate the immensity of the land. He reflects on the disproportion between the effort and work of the ploughmen and the harvest they take in, and he sympathizes with the small, submissive men, barefooted but wearing peaked caps, who bend over their furrows working day after day. The land has etched an indelible impression on Mao Tse-tung's memory, just as the spectacle of the factories left its mark on most of the Soviet revolutionaries.

One of the first poems that Mao wrote was called "Peace." In it he compared peace with the starry sky and with the tiny boats that move in and out among the junks. The first newspaper he founded was called "Critic of the New Hunan"; it died with neither pity nor glory. And then one day the young catechumen discovered in the University shelves of books on Western philosophy, more modern than

Lao-tse and Confucius: Montesquieu, Rousseau, Marx, Engels, Lenin. . . .

The intricate doctrine of Marx, who was a lawyer's son, became dogma for Mao Tse-tung, especially in regard to economic factors and the class struggle. For his own part, Mao saw dynastic China in a process of decomposition. He could not understand why vast stretches of the country were untouched wasteland, why capital and labor should forever be at each other's throats, and why the Chinese women's feet should still be tightly bound to make them tiny. To his way of thinking, the whole structure of society was one big sin of selfishness, lack of cohesion, and foolishness, offering no appreciable resistance to the whims of nature.

And then he recalled Confucius' maxim about the superior man, and began to examine himself. He felt strong, "absolute master of his thoughts," to such an extent that he rebelled; he rebelled so much that in 1919, at the age of twenty-six, he took part for the first time in a revolutionary act: the protest movement against Japan's territorial demands. Japan was to be a perpetual grain of sand in his eye.

Mao was married in 1920, the same year that the first cell of the Communist Party was founded in China. He married a young student named Yang Kai-hui, who was killed ten years later by Mao's eternal adversaries, the Nationalists. He married again, but this second marriage ended in divorce. According to his own declarations, from that time in 1939 on, ". . . I was to find but one method of escape from loneliness: serving the Communist Party and China with all my might."

Very early Mao Tse-tung showed himself to be a born leader. His knowledge of English and of Western politics gave him an automatic advantage over his comrades. His appearance had nothing military about it, as was the case with his mortal enemy, Chiang Kai-shek. He still looked like an easy-going but sly peasant, with a dash of the school teacher about him. However, now that his health was better, his interior energy was indomitable. He subjected himself to a strict discipline which included everything from studying into the small hours of the morning—often sitting on the stairs, one of Lenin's favorite positions—to cold showers when it was freezing outside; "Cold showers," he said, "are a whip which tames the bones of the human body."

In 1921 he took part in the first national convention of the Communist Party, then made up of fifty-seven members, the majority of them intellectuals. In 1924 he was a delegate to the first national convention of the Kuomintang and shortly afterwards became director of the Shanghai Communist newspaper.

This was Mao Tse-tung's critical moment. He had two courses open to him: he could choose to follow the orders of the Russian Communist Party blindly or, on the other hand, to subordinate them to the realities of China. He chose the latter course, against the wishes of the founder of the Party himself, Chen Tu-hsiu, professor at the University of Peking. Mao, from the vantage point afforded him by the paper, bravely insisted on the radical distinction between Russia and China. In Russia, the victors of the October Revolution found themselves the rulers of a nation with a considerable mass of workers; in China 85 per cent of the population was made up of illiterate peasants, farmers, subjected to the feudal control of the war lords, "tuchuns," who reigned in their individual provinces like viceroys or princes. These peasants lacked even a fighting spirit; they feared the miserable land which nourished them so poorly, were paralyzed by superstition, and farmed by the most rudimentary methods.

According to Mao, who before beginning his work in Shanghai had travelled China from one end to the other, from Tibet to Tonkin and from the Gobi Desert to Outer Mongolia, the situation called for an adaptation of the traditional methods used in Russia. "Addressing a factory worker dressed in blue overalls and boots is not the same as addressing some poor untouchable, sunk up to his waist in a swampy rice field." "Unless the Party refocuses and solves the agrarian problem, it will be such a failure that all Asia will be lost to Communism." It was a thesis at once logical and temperamental. Factories suffocated Mao, as he was later to confess. He preferred a crackling camp-fire in the forest, with its mysterious and fragrant smoke, to factory smokestacks, which struck him as all alike, foolishly rigid and inviting sabotage.

The paper that Mao put out in Shangai became the champion of this idea; it was an implacable and penetrating stand, and its originality consisted in the fact that his choice of words was both academic and rustic. Mao loved to use country metaphors or, in lieu of them, sea expressions. Among the numerous little groups of people that met regularly to exchange commentaries on the passing scene, the paper was always read aloud, with considerable relish, and invariably drew murmurs of assent. It circulated from hand to hand and reached readers even far from Shanghai. People began to use the phrase which later on would be repeated endlessly: "At least he is offering us something. . . ."

Mao's attitude earned him the reputation of being a "revisionist," in view of the fact that Marx had written that peasants were an "inert and conservative element" and the fact that Lenin himself had established the principle that the Revolution must begin with the working classes. Mao did not allow himself to be budged an inch: "The only means of achieving victory is by carrying out agrarian reform."

Victory over whom? Over General Chiang Kai-shek, Mao's most obstinate rival, so obstinate that after several decades the two of them are still on their feet and nominally at war, one in Peking and the other in Formosa.

It was about that time that the Chiang group made a trip to Russia and returned singing the praises of Soviet organization, but at the same time condemning the doctrine, "a cold doctrine, which subjugates man-value to collectivity-value." One of the results of the trip was that Chiang declared the Chinese Communist Party illegal—a slap in the face for Mao—and another was his announcement of great plans for China's future, based mainly on industrialization and the emancipation of women. Chiang's wife, Mei-ling Soong, was to play a decisive role in the preparation and implementation of all these projects; she exercised an enormous influence over him, to the point where she converted him to Methodism and convinced him that God had given the two of them a mission to complete in China.

Chiang called Mao a "whitened sepulcher" and a "hyena dressed in Pekinese cat's clothing." In all honesty, it is doubtful that he could ever have imagined him as China's future leader. On the other hand, Mao, while despising Chiang Kai-shek as a protector of the trusts and English banking system, gave him and his wife their due. "Together, they represent a force," he observed. "They are speculating at China's expense on the country's weariness. Cutting off their heads won't be an easy job."

Naturally, Mao was still a long way from being official leader of the Communist Party at that time. The leader named by Moscow was Chen Tu-hsiu. Mao's revolutionary program, which consisted of gaining control of the rural areas, conflicted with Chen Tu-hsiu's orthodoxy; his idea was to foment uprisings in the big cities like Canton, Wuchang and Changsha, in the hope of gaining support among the masses of workers. The rift between the two leaders became wider and more dramatic, until at last they agreed on only one thing: the necessity of fighting Chiang Kai-shek, to the point of civil war if need be. The pacifism of Lao-tse was left far behind—"Let us abandon things to themselves and not carry them to extremes," he had said —and in its place appeared the Soviet thesis that ultimate Socialist world victory depended on winning over the Orient, especially China's and India's gigantic populations, to the revolutionary movement begun by Soviet Russia.

Events seemed to prove that Mao was right. Chen Tu-hsiu undertook a Marxist assault on the cities and was mercilessly crushed by Chiang's military machine. The workers he managed to mobilize displayed an embarrassing rashness and painful lack of revolutionary nerve. Their failure was spectacular and complete all over China, like a chain reaction. The government newspapers had a field day ridiculing them and even in the theaters their quixotic rebellion was lampooned in numerous parodies.

The blow dealt to the Communist Party appeared mortal. The Kremlin itself seemed to abandon it as a lost cause. Perhaps those who had said that something racial, something profound in China, opposed Marxism's advance were right after all. Among them was Gandhi, so anxious to extend his Hindu doctrine of non-violence across Asia.

It was then that Mao Tse-tung gave a demonstration of what he was made of, of his revolutionary skill. Taking with him the remnant of the Party that had remained loyal, he moved to the country, to the district of Kiangsi. So great was his self-confidence that he declared that Chiang Kai-shek's days were numbered, a declaration which produced amazement among even his own followers. Chiang, with the reins of power firmly in hand, laughed in his face but Mao did not budge. He continued to take cold showers daily and to tell anyone who would listen that Communism had an intrinsic force capable of winning any battle, however unmatched it might appear. "Chiang Kai-shek has guns but I have faith," he stated. Between guns and faith, China was soon swept into a civil war; the little group following Mao would keep on growing until it formed a resistance force capable of meeting Chiang's troops face to face. All Mao's verses about the starry sky and the little boats moving in and out among the junks had been left far behind on some classroom desk in his elementary school. In a short time thousands of huts were to go up in flames and men were to be busy killing one another.

At the outset the "troops" that Mao managed to gather together in the Kiangsi region were comical and a bit pitiful. They were few in number, with hardly any arms, and given over to the most contentious sort of anarchy. Coolie hats were mixed in with army helmets and jockey caps like Mao wore. There were baggy trousers and shorts, all kinds of kimonos and multicolored shirts floating in the breeze. To complete the picture, there were plenty of bare feet and bandaged limbs, souvenirs of the skirmishes in the cities. Mao was constantly passing among his men like a man possessed, finding an encouraging and inspiring word for each of them. His habits were those of a despot, with a touch of the benevolent father about him. He was deeply concerned with sanitation and set up medical dispensaries in all the areas he occupied. Unexpectedly, he showed a willingness to permit women and children to join the troops: "The fight will be a long one," he told his militiamen, "and I am afraid of the consequences of loneliness." What was going to happen? What was Mao's objective?

Mao's objective was worthy of a madman; it consisted of advancing across practically the entire map of China, toward the north, until the frontier region of Yenan was reached. This was a total of almost seven thousand miles! The expedition was to proceed on foot at a forced march and try at all costs to avoid clashes with Chiang Kai-shek's forces. Obviously, despite their lovely colors, the maps described in no uncertain terms what this would involve: passing eighteen mountain chains, crossing twenty-four rivers, going around fifty-two cities . . . . the whole undertaking seemed almost mythological. Seven thousand miles! Fortunately, Mao's lucky star stayed with him; after all, he had been born in the month of the Green Rat, on the day of the Red Rooster, at the hour of the Dragon. . . .

This weird caravan, made up of some hundred thousand adventurers, finally got under way in the year 1934. In all the history of emigration it stands alone as an unprecedented feat of daring; later on it was to be spoken of as "The Long March." During the course of this march, Mao was going to have to face ten different armed corps sent against him by Chiang Kai-shek and he would lose two-thirds of the initial convoy. Only about thirty thousand were to reach their goal, the Yenan region; the rest would desert or die on the way.

Throughout his odyssey, Mao was constantly seeking recruits. His stratagem consisted in ordering his men to take part in whatever happened to be the agricultural chore of the moment; this afforded a perfect excuse to initiate a dialogue with the peasants, even tnough many of them stood as dumb as statues on hearing the word "Moscow." What the devil did that mean? What did "Moscow" have to do with China? Other peasants, on the contrary, were most receptive to Mao's promises to distribute the land, provide machinery and chemical fertilizers, and get rid of the war lords, landowners, and the many government parasites clustered around Chiang in Peking. What was this exciting program called? There was but one name for it: Socialism. It was a recent discovery, a sort of natural miracle, a fabulous medicine with the power to equalize rights and opportunities; on contact, it eliminated illiteracy, contagious diseases, and even sadness.

Mao's popularity increased day by day, reaching the furthermost corners of the land. Everyone talked of "The Long March." At times there were rumors that the caravan had been completely wiped out, but such was not the case. The expedition would always disprove these rumors with some new sign of life; it was always a little further to the north, a little closer to Yenan. Actually, the situation had developed into a real war, in which Mao behaved like a real military expert in strategy and tactics. Chiang Kai-shek, who closely followed on his maps the masterful evacuation maneuver, eventually offered a quarter of a million dollars for Mao's head; Mao, with his customary psychological alertness, replied by offering one dollar for Chiang's head!

China's future was in the balance, even though no one fully realized the operation's importance at the time. If Chiang Kai-shek, a convert to Christianity, won the struggle, then China would have a clear field ahead in her alignment with the West. However, if Mao Tse-tung and his forces won, the Kremlin would back him up in a revolutionary situation whose outcome would be difficult to predict.

The forces fighting under Mao had no doubt that he would remain firm. He was a living proof of the power of energy mixed with cold calculation. He seemed to know all the dialects, all the customs, all the anxieties and superstitions of the regions he passed through. He left behind him in every spot he visited an aura of intelligence and good will; however, if the enemy showed up he also left behind a pile of corpses.

Photos of that period show a robust Mao, with a soft expression full of "goodness." Mao's "goodness" has always been very photogenic. Observers at the time underlined the extraordinary complexity of his temperament. Implacable with the enemy, he felt great pity toward the most insignificant wounded soldier, as well as toward animals, especially dogs and cats. He could condemn people to death without blinking an eyelash and a moment later stare absently at the surrounding countryside through his binoculars. Rain did not affect him in the least; he let the rain pour down on him without paying any attention to it. If the sun shone, he went to sit down in the nearest hut or under a tree, fanning himself and writing verses—Mao never left off being the poet. During that period, stimulated by his open-air life, he wrote a book called *Poems of the Earth and the Wind* in which he frequently spoke of the bamboo plant. He was attracted to bamboo in a special way because it was China's most abundant raw material, found everywhere, like Chiang's troops. He also wrote of the cold that swept down from Siberia, of bears and of ants. He liked to recite his own verses, with all the thousand and one inflections which the Chinese dialects require. He often did so around a campfire while the members of his escort sat about eating with chopsticks, and up above the moon bathed the oriental landscape in a soft melancholy.

At last, toward the end of 1935, Mao reached the frontier region of Yenan. It was an arid land with a difficult climate and many eroded rocks; there it was that Mao set up his general headquarters. The hollows or caves in the rocks became living quarters, like gypsy caves. The territory soon bulged with more than a million inhabitants, whom Mao was to govern with absolute power.

He decided to set up a military dictatorship in the new community; its officials were selected from among the survivors of The Long March and Yenan's inhabitants became citizen-soldiers. The former gave orders and exercised control while the latter alternated their respective jobs or professions with military training, which consisted not only in rifle drill and instruction in the use of hand grenades but also vigilance in the field, in the workshop, and even in the family circle, in order to expose enemies of the dictatorship. The official theory was that a good number of these enemies could be "rehabilitated" through work; stubborn cases were handed over to the firing squads, made up of a handful of militiamen named on the spot. Yenan turned into a "state within a state," a throwback to the caveman age, judging by the number of caves used as dwellings and the organization of social life. However, in its womb—Mao's residence—the new China was taking shape, a China which would throw herself into the Marxist frenzy with more abandon than even the Soviet Union.

Yenan became, too, the sanctuary or first cell of the Chinese Communist era, with plenty of time for study and contemplation. Mao Tse-tung, unquestionably the boss, future master of China, established in Yenan's caves the bases for the present revolution. His books, *The New Democracy* and *On a Coalition Government,* were written in Yenan, and in Yenan he announced that, after his triumph over Chiang, China's evolution would be composed of three stages: first, the New Democracy; second, Socialism; lastly, Communism. In Yenan Mao declared that Communism was a total undertaking, a way of life which affected all of life's forms and aspects, and that in China it would profoundly affect all of the nation's institutions, influencing everything from the interpretation of Tao, "the Way," to the manner of honoring the dead and preparing tea.

Some of the sayings from the Yenan days have come down to us across the years: "War is the most elevated form of the class struggle"; "Political power comes from the muzzle of a gun"; "Activity is the highest form of happiness." Later on, after he had seized power, Mao was to apply these catchwords to the whole country on a gigantic scale.

In Yenan Mao carried out two kinds of experiments: experiments of liberation and others of renunciation. Those of liberation were centered around the awakening of the Chinese woman, which coincided with the objective of Madame Chiang Kai-shek, and the integration of children and adolescents into the work of the Revolution. The experiments of renunciation centered around seminars which accomplished a kind of brainwashing, and the establishment of audacious "People's Communes."

The job of liberating the Chinese woman met with great difficulties right from the start, since it aggressively went against the most deeply rooted Chinese traditions. Mao went even further, mobilizing the women militarily and making them take part in all sorts of work and exercises, whether or not compatible with feminine physiology. All this was a flagrant contradiction of what Mao had written in his youth: "Women is like the wing of a bird, like a seed-pod one must fondly tend, like quiet waters." A seed-pod with rifle! A bird's wing driving ten-ton trucks and working in the coal mines! The women in Yenan were no longer quiet waters; they were torrents, and perhaps it was for this reason that many of them churned up a timid but indignant foam. There were all sorts of reactions: some were enthusiastic in their adhesion to the new covenant, others felt inadequate to the challenge, still others lapsed into anguish and even suicide. But the reactions did not matter. The goal was set and yet to be achieved: "Two arms stretched out to a child are but two arms," Mao had said, "but two arms in the field or in a factory are two pillars of the Revolution."

As for the inclusion of adolescents, it was explained that Marx had asked: "Why not use child labor?" The next step was obvious. Mao furnished the children with rifles and spades; with the rifles they stood guard on the hilltops and with the spades they pitched in with the farming chores. They also took part in transportation work. The children's reactions were in general more favorable than the women's, since they had the feeling they were useful and this stimulated them. They sang and laughed. Mao spoke of his "great success" and the "happy beehive." He organized all sorts of contests and competitions, usually of physical exercise and kite-flying, and awarded the prizes himself; they ranged from a medal and a furlough to visit one's family to the privilege of sitting at Mao's table and even of serving in his personal honor-guard. The youngsters in this honor guard were all matched according to height, and hovered over their leader as though he were God Himself. They were infused with a fanatical esprit de corps. Gradually these adolescent military units assumed an almost comical air of self-importance and developed an uncontrollable hunger for violence and power.

The experiments in renunciation were carried out through the creation of People's Communes, seminars for the formation of young leaders, the systematic collection of excrement for fertilizing the crops, etc., all of which implied a much more intense and indescribable adventure. The object of the People's Communes was to eliminate family life in the towns and villages, replacing it with collective life. Everyone worked in a group, ate together in canteens, and slept in big hanger-like quonsets, with the children living in cooperative nurseries and the old people in so-called "Happiness Houses." Former living quarters were emptied out and used as warehouses or workshops. The new schedule consisted of a thirteen hour work-day, with additional hours of indoctrination at Party headquarters nightly and periodic meetings between the men and women, closely patrolled and with a rigid time-limit. The only thing that mattered was production. The main guide and point of reference was the production graph which was hung up at the end of the day. Mao walked through the streets every evening studying these charts, with no thought for the state of physical and spiritual exhaustion they implied. The important thing was not the present but tomorrow, in conformity with the Communist theory that it is important to strangle the concept of time and replace it with the concept of the common good.

The seminars were training courses for the formation of teams of youth leaders—the minority who would later have to set the example and tend the sacred fire. The program in these courses was exhausting and allowed scarcely any time at all for relaxation. As in brainwashing, involved were a revision of one's past life, self-analysis, a confession of guilt, informing on one's friends, etc. In this area Mao obtained enviable success. Burdened from time immemorial by a sterile history which had not managed to free China from slavery and want, the young people of Yenan chosen for the program (the "Kun Pa" seminars) gave themselves body and soul to the new system. Two indispensable requirements were physical vigor and a certain coldness. Those who stood the test were, within a few months, able to watch calmly the execution of countless "reactionaries," and at the same time were prepared to betray any truth without the slightest scruple or invent out of thin air any fact that might happen to fit into their pre-arranged scheme. As with yoga, the strength of the Kun-Pa courses lay in self-control, in an asceticism capable of turning sacrifice and even pain into enjoyment. These young leaders accomplished real feats of daring, difficult and painful assignments, with a strange smile on their lips. Naturally, Mao placed his main hope in them and made them repeat frequently a brief dialogue which soon became famous:

"Communism is love," said one young man.

"No, comrade," replied his companion. "Communism is the hammer we use to destroy the enemy."

Mao's fame and that of his remote settlement spread all over the country. News filtered out like water seeping from a bamboo basket. Mao could not rely on the organized support of his comrades spread out through all the big cities, because these comrades had been dispersed by Chiang's troops two years earlier. Nevertheless, the Communist cells—and they were all over China—joined in a chorus of warm praise for the movement in Yenan, weaving about the Party a romantic aura which a certain sector of the people responded to. It can easily be said that by 1936 the civil war between Mao Tse-tung and Chiang Kai-shek had completely engrossed the nation's attention. One minute the rumor was circulating that Mao had succeeded in making the land around his little community give three crops per year, and the next minute people were hinting that Soviet doctors had arrived in Yenan and were teaching the women a method of painless childbirth. People also spoke of certain terrible secret weapons in Mao's possession. The slightest wavering on Chiang's part or any unexpected trip he made was at once interpreted as a sign of fear or weakness.

Mao had already achieved one victory: China was talking about Communism and becoming interested in its doctrine, everyone according to his own interests and needs. The artisans, a group with an ancient reputation and tradition, spoke with misgivings about the New Law which intended to establish a system of mass production, socialized, of course. The needy jumped to all sorts of conclusions, based on the pathetic idea that ". . . at least Mao was offering something" and on a belief in "equality of opportunity." Among the intellectuals there were many who sympathized with the Party, who admired Mao and predicted that his victory in China was inevitable. Mme. Chiang Kai-shek felt that these intellectuals were right in guessing that Communism would eventually win, since China was the only Asiatic nation lacking the strong, unifying religious creed which could possibly oppose it. "Confucianism, the worship of Tao and Buddhism constitute ethical and moral codes and even some measure of rites, but they lack the indispensable supernatural ingredient that would make their believers ready to give their very lives to defend them," she stated. "Consequently, we see no other solution for stopping Mao except the use of arms, carrying the Civil War to its ultimate conclusion."

Mao sensed that what the Party lacked was the opportunity of winning the hearts of the masses. Again, fate was kind to him. Such an opportunity presented itself in 1937 with the Japanese offensive along China's northern frontier. A compact resistance movement sprang up in several provinces, with the purpose of ". . . doing away with the internal struggle in order to unite all the opposed forces and concentrate them against Japan." Mao gave another sample of his lightning-fast reflexes: he was the first to come out enthusiastically in favor of the patriotic idea. "For my part," he promised, "I'd be ready to offer my own troops to General Chiang Kai-shek."

To the amazement of both intimates and strangers, Chiang accepted this offer, and Mao, escorted by the veterans of The Long March and the young people trained in the Kun-Pa centers, shouted: "Forward!" His cry resounded throughout a great sector of the nation and buoyed up people's spirits. Before long the Eighth Campaign Army was in operation; this Army, under Mao's orders, promptly went into action against the advance Japanese guard and its behavior was exemplary. The soldiers of the Eighth Campaign Army covered themselves with glory on the battle field, to the point that Chaing Kai-shek himself wound up nicknaming them "The Red Dragons."

Mao had found the ideal element, the missing link. His army was constantly growing, swollen by the peasants pouring in from the country. The squalid and fugitive caravan of The Long March and the embryonic rehearsal in the Yenan region had been transformed into a raging torrent of a million soldiers, equipped for war and disciplined,

who mixed military action with propaganda and made it
their business to leave in their wake a strategic assortment
of revolutionary seeds. The leader corps, finished products
of the Kun-Pa, had begun to go into action.

The rest unwound slowly and with an implacable logic.
Upon the Japanese surrender in 1945, signed aboard the
heavily armored warship "Missouri," Mao made public his
decision not to give up an inch of the land conquered by
his "Red Dragons." Chiang Kai-shek, although knowing
himself to be backed up by the Western powers, could not
disguise his fear. He knew the monolithic force of Mao's
doctrine as well as his annoying elasticity. Moreover,
Chiang realized that his position with regard to Mao was
unfavorable. Actually, it was enough for Mao to be faithful
to the unvarying tactics of the Party, which consisted on
one hand of letting the enemy's mistakes mount up and,
on the other, of making up a long and tantalizing list of
promises to the people. From his state within a state Mao
could with impunity promise hydroelectric projects, highways, the union of all the Chinese people, happiness;
Chiang, on the contrary, had to act with tangible and immediate efficiency. He had to supply the nation's necessities, undertake war repairs, reorganize industry and
agriculture, bury the dead, etc.

Chaing Kai-shek, despite the untiring help of his wife,
whose name, Mei-ling Soong, means "magnificent character" in Chinese, did not succeed in averting the danger.
He lacked the personal authority and political vision necessary to solve the infinite problems of the most densely pop-
ulated nation on earth. He made many mistakes: among
them, that of once again basing his agrarian reform on the
big landholder system—a mistake so many make—and per-
mitting the internal administration of his government to go

on becoming more and more scandalously corrupt. But the greatest lack was elsewhere. He was unable to offer China a centrifugal and popular doctrine which, like Communism, would involve a global conception of life.

The resuts were not long in appearing. Mao's position soon became so strong that Chiang had no choice but to intensify the pathetic calls for help he had been sending off to the West for some time. Mao Tse-tung, ever alert, promptly followed the same tactic and appealed to Russia, whom he called his "elder sister," for help. "In order to guarantee the Party's victory in China you ought to be willing to melt down even the Kremlin walls to make guns. The future of Asia is in the balance." The reactions were quite different. The West hesitated, but Russia, on the other hand, turned over to Mao all the armaments the Japanese had left behind when they retreated from Manchuria.

This development speeded up Mao's victorious advance; his promises were soothing to the Chinese, so fed up with official evasion of problems. "We know what Chiang Kaishek can give us," people had begun to say. The Chinese were looking for a different kind of experience, a cohesive factor which would size up their problems with honesty.

Mao's lieutenants realized that only one piece was lacking to complete the great pyramid: the glorification of their leader, his deification in the eyes of the masses.

This became the next big project. Newspapers like the one Mao had run in Shanghai sprang up everywhere, along with pictures of the Chinese Communist leader, the ex-assistant librarian at the University of Peking. All sorts of pictures of Mao were circulated: big photos and little ones, on cardboard backing, on fans, on lamp shades and stuck on the back of trucks. Lapel buttons bearing his portrait and plaster busts were turned out by the thousands and on all of them Mao's expression was kind and benevolent, befitting a "father of his country." People began to talk about the "Mao Tse-tung era," pointing out that the happy future that he predicted was a perfectly identifiable and earthly future. "Mao doesn't promise us pie in the sky, but instead a great China right here on earth." "Mao is not a charlatan, he is a political organizer." Unexpectedly, he found protectors in the most unlikely places: among the members of the British colony in Hong Kong, for example. In his propaganda pictures, Mao was usually accompanied by Chou En-lai, the executor of his doctrine, as well as by his two sisters, simple women who lovingly cared for him in his solitude.

Madame Chiang Kai-shek turned out to be right. The struggle was dramatic, stubborn, and full of surprises but in the end Mao won out. His ultimate and decisive victory took place in January of 1949, just twenty-nine years after the founding of the country's first Communist cell.

The paradoxical Chiang moved to Formosa with his wife and a few thousand Nationalist followers while Mao, the leader who had gathered together some one hundred thirty thousand half-naked troops in 1934, who condemned people to death without batting an eyelash, and who wrote verses about the bears and the ants, ascended the Imperial Throne in Peking's Summer Palace, proclaiming the Chinese People's Republic. As was expected, he became the most powerful man on the Asian continent, a living reincarnation of the ancient emperors whom the Chinese had venerated as "agents of the Most High."

Mao's triumph may be considered as a triumph of tenaciousness at the service of revolutionary genius; but in spite of this, China was to go on being what it had always been since time immemorial: a valley of tears.

3

———◆———

THE REVOLUTION IN ACTION

Mao's behavior once he became the leader of the Chinese people was from the first moment spectacular and energetic. For one thing, he prosecuted the government officials who had grown poppies and exported opium, and for another he renamed streets and monuments with all sorts of provocative titles: "Boulevard of Peaceful Long Life," "Temple of Supreme Harmony," "Pavillion of Never-broken Peace," etc. In addition to sending messages to the wealthy Chinese living abroad, requesting donations to "ensure the safety of relatives still in China," he also set in motion an enthusiastic movement for the renovation of the Chinese popular theatre.

In step with Mao, China experienced a moment of delirium; at night one could hear in the rice paddies and on the tea plantations sounds never before heard. The cohesive element the Chinese people had been clamoring for was given them at last. Nature had supplied China with a vital leader who seemed to have learned a lesson from Hitler and Mussolini, with their bloody ends to their careers; he had hung up in his office a gold-engraved motto which said: "The furious man has no eyes." Mao seemed never to become furious. His main characteristic, in fact, was his serenity. Mao's serenity contrasted sharply with Stalin's proud disdain and Lenin's violent rages.

Mao never forgot Stalin's fundamental advice, which was that a Communist dictatorship ought to take over complete control of the army, the police and the administration of justice. These three main pillars of a dictator were already under his control. As far as the army was concerned, he could reply on his "Red Dragons" and the heroic legend they had engraved on the hearts of the people. As for the police, he had thousands of volunteer sentinels at his disposal, all members of the Party. And finally, in the question of justice, he had formed "people's courts" immediately and was also counting on the latent desire for revenge common to all the Celestial Empire. Furthermore, he was familiar with the sayings of the Jacobins during the French Revolution: "It is necessary to punish not only the traitors but the indifferent as well." In other words, the first step consisted in the elimination of the visible enemy; after that, the next step would be to exterminate the invisible enemy. It was a violent but delicate operation which would settle the question once and for all.

Among the first measures Mao took was a strictly practical one: a census of the Chinese population. Until then the censuses had been of families, not of individuals, a clear indication of the dominant patriarchal makeup of the nation. Mao broke the old pattern. He wanted to know the exact number of troops available to him. It was by no means an easy job, in view of the many ethnic minorities

living in far-off places like the Gobi Desert, in the Ma-
laysian provinces, in Chang-Pai, in the Gulf of Tonkin.
The census was completed at last, however, and from that
moment Mao decreed that for the first time in many decades
the same civil and military law would apply to all the
Chinese. What is more, he succeeded in extracting from
them a certain conformity, a reverence for the super-state
above all else. Mao's slogan continued to be the same:
"Union creates strength, a strength made of iron, a strength
made of steel."

Mao promptly took advantage of the situation to create
a climate of fanatical nationalism. The majority of foreigners living in China who were not imprisoned were expelled and their property confiscated. The cry of "China
for the Chinese!" was heard once more, and the emphasis
on precision in weights and measures, dates and numbers,
so beloved by the Chinese, was restored; this time, though,
it was joyfully directed toward a better future. All the nation's traditions were closely examined, looking for rocks
which blocked the road forward. Many superstitions were
uprooted, like the practice of sleeping kneeling up during
pregnancy to implore the gods' protection, or of not fixing
up tumble-down buildings for fear of angering the elements.
Several of the most ancient libraries in China went up in
flames and only those books were saved which might be
considered useful in some way to the Revolution, like the
poems of Chu Yuan. Many classical poems, which were
written without a thought of the collectivity, were now
rewritten and given the proper slant.

This fanatical exaltation of nationalism stirred up sincere
enthusiasm, not only because the recent Japanese occupa-
tion had left incurable wounds, but because an innate sentiment, surpressed for generations as the result of poverty,

favored such a severe xenophobia. The idea that China might become self-sufficient thanks to the "new winds" that were blowing in her favor made everyone's face brighten. From Peking to the remotest village every flagpole flew the banner of the Celestial Empire, made out of the most unlikely materials. And all the while the eternal choruses of Chinese chanted: "Everything the eye can see is ours and no one will take it away from us."

The second measure that Mao adopted was repression. His methods were worthy of a Herod and led some to speculate about the supposed Chinese inclination toward deceit and cruelty. The first victims were the big landholders and former Chiang collaborators. After that came the bankers, industrialists, and business men. Next, the professional men, especially doctors, who had not demonstrated a spontaneous support of the People's Revolution. Finally, the last victims were the countless thousands of tormented Chinese whose only crime had been their difficulty in getting used to the new conditions created by the Revolution.

The law courts were staffed by ordinary citizens; this was the highest title in the new state, "Ordinary Citizen." The only requirement necessary for sitting on the judges' bench was to have an accusation of usury or mistreatment against someone, even though the offense might have taken place twenty years before. Actually, all accusations were valid, and there was no need to offer any proof. Especially well received were the accusations of women scorned and those of children.

Executions were usually public. Among the most popular sites were stadiums and sports arenas, especially the former dog-track in Shanghai. Other popular places for holding executions were public squares, crossroads, the courtyards of confiscated Buddhist temples, river banks, and property boundary-lines. Furious masses of people took part in these executions; in the twinkling of an eye they went from terror to sardonic smiles. Many children and, of course, relatives were obliged to be present at the executions. After they were over there was a great silence, broken suddenly by a band that began to play or by an anthem sung by the Party leaders. The most frequently used means of execution were a shot in the back of the head, the gallows, and strangulation.

The third measure adopted by Mao was propaganda. China was turned into a gigantic amphitheatre where there was one big parade or rally after another, always presided over by the veterans of The Long March and by an ironic emblem—Picasso's peace dove! All through this propaganda there were frequent references to the nation's great population wealth and its people's capacity for expansion. The writings of Mao and Stalin were widely distributed together, and a special commission was set up to influence children's minds. Mao did not forget the well-known Chinese proverb: "If you are planning for a few years, plant grain. If you are planning for a decade, plant trees. But if you are planning for a century, educate men."

The fourth step that Mao took was to announce to the nation a gigantic public-works project which he had been promising for some time, which would include the Peking Subway—a copy of the one in Moscow—and the taming of the Hwang Ho or Yellow River, known as "China's Great Sorrow"; the latter project was to become the backbone of the grand plan of rebirth. The dimensions and details of this plan astonished the Chinese. Nothing had escaped Mao's zeal for renovation; he had no permanent residence and seemed to be everywhere at once.

Naturally, there was no scarcity of sceptical theoreticians, both inside and outside of China, who ventured to say that the castle Mao was building would come tumbling down in nothing flat for lack of stability, but he made fun of these prophets, whom he called crows. "China is poised to make the Great Leap Forward, and the crows' predictions of doom will not stop us," he said. The people were already dressing in blue coveralls and jockey caps and singing:

> Leader Mao is infinitely good,
> Ten thousand praises would not be
> enough to honor him.
> With trees for pens,
> The sky for paper
> And the sea for ink,
> Much would still remain to be written.

At that moment, March of 1950, Mao was putting the finishing touches to a vitally important agreement with Stalin. Mao considered Stalin to be at the peak of his career as a practical, useful ruler. "If we study Marxism," he declared on his return from Moscow, "It is not because of its beautiful literature, nor because it has any magic capable of charming the devil. Let us understand once and for all that Marxism is neither magical nor beautiful, but simply useful."

The pact involved massive technical and industrial assistance on Russia's part, the establishment of extensive rail and air links between the two countries, and the preparation of a huge standing Chinese army which would permit Mao to occupy Tibet and other adjacent regions within a short time. In exchange, China would agree to refrain from any deviationist or revisionist tendencies—how the tables have turned!—and would send her Kun-Pa students to Moscow for final training; she would also send periodic shipments of food to Russia. This last point illustrates the confidence that Mao had in his agrarian reform.

This Russian alliance led Mao to new extremes in his anti-Western campaign: France was condemned for her colonialism in Indo-China; England, for her colonialism in India; Germany, for her "claim that the Arian race is superior to the Chinese race," etc. Party speakers went to great pains to display their pride that China did so many things contrary to the way they were done in the West; for example, that books were read from back to front, that lines were written from right to left, that one shook hands with oneself, that the simple act of sitting down was filled with exquisite ceremony and care. "Westerners don't dress as we do, and don't love kites and paper lanterns." "In Western society people don't know how to smoke, and there are all sorts of crimes of passion." "Westerners dirty their handkerchiefs and then keep them in their pockets for days on end."

This campaign, encouraged by Stalin, "China's best friend," reached its zenith at the time of the Korean War, which enabled Mao to prove to the people his fervent nationalism and his contempt for the United States. Chinese soldiers died on the battle field, with their "Red Dragon" medals on their chests. A tremendous wave of hatred for the West swept across the nation. It was said that the United States was even waging bacteriological warfare, which made the entire population shudder with horror. In toy shops there were special books in which the children signed their names as a demonstration of their hatred for the United States, and in school plays and pageants, so popular among Chinese children, there were many scenes of uniformed children firing at American planes. Statements like the following one were printed in instruction manuals and newspapers: "In the United States there are blood banks belonging to ambitious professionals who will stop at nothing to make a profit; they even take blood from unemployed workers, not just figuratively but literally."

In the field of practical accomplishments Mao's first concern was the creation of a mystique of work. The publicity campaign and the pressure exerted to achieve this goal were called the "Imposition of Correct Thinking." It was a psychological operation designed to transform completely the Chinese, until then conservative and anarchistic, into a collective social unit responsible for community life.

All of this had to be built upon the most solid base possible: a mystique of work. Mao came up with just the right slogan: "Nature and the normal course of events have for centuries decided our fate; now, for the first time, we are the ones who will decide the course of events and determine our own future." The immense public-works project previously announced, without precedents even in Pharaonic times, was at last put into operation. "We shall convert China into one gigantic blast furnace, and at the same time a flowering orchard," promised Mao. The Chinese people, who called the cold winds from the north "ancestors' wrath," closed ranks shoulder to shoulder, ready to tame nature. Every big city founded its Worker's Palace and opened permanent work expositions. The blue cotton coverall became standard dress all over China. If a factory boosted production, a brass band paraded through the streets proclaiming the happy fact. Those workers who broke production records were awarded prizes of medals and little red flags or had their pictures printed on match books. On the trains, loudspeakers repeated over and over again: "A pick in one hand and a rifle in the other." Chou En-lai declared that China ought to walk with both legs, that is to say, develop both agriculture and industry. In order to make the Great Leap Forward a success, it would be necessary to duplicate the feats of the construction of the Grand Canal, the Pyramids and the Great Wall of China.

The first five-year plan was launched, timed to coincide with the arrival of the Russian technicians and equipment promised by Stalin. The daily Moscow-Peking Express was christened "The Train of Efficient Aid" in honor of these technicians.

This five-year plan was divided into campaigns which would serve to keep public enthusiasm alive month after month and year after year. The first one was the "Bursting Forth of Factories," which quickly turned into a great success. Within a short time all sorts of smokestacks sprang up alongside the rivers. The new slogan was: "A few years of effort and a thousand years of happiness." At the same time, numerous teams of geologists were sent off to the farthest corners of the land to investigate mineral wealth. The smoke from the smokestacks was visible for miles and dazzled the peasants and farmers working in the fields; after their work was over for the day they often thronged into the factories to stare at the marvelous, shiny new machinery which was going to redeem China by turning out railway cars and trucks, antibiotics and precision instruments.

The method used in quickly putting up huge industrial plants was quite simple: the massive use of manpower, a manpower whose silent obedience and self-sacrifice made up for the lack of construction equipment and transport. It was not unusual for this popular contribution to sometimes achieve miracles, such as was the case in the steel drive. The number of blast furnaces was insufficient and Chou En-lai had said: "Steel is the heart of prosperity." Before you could say "five-year plan" thousands upon thousands of homemade furnaces blossomed everywhere: in the streets, in patios, in vacant lots. They were made of bricks at first and, later on, with scraps of steel also. The women immediately gave them poetic names, like: "Hearts of Fire," "Red Hands," "Pank-Ou's Yawns" ((Pank-Ou was the legendary giant who had created China). Whenever a village or city ran out of raw materials, people did not hesitate to chip in anything they could: kitchen utensils, tables and chairs, tools, the radiators from churches. . . .

Industrialization was on such an immense scale that the metaphor of the ants and bees seemed ridiculously inadequate to describe it; the great industrial complexes at Anshan, Wuhan and Pactow were soon going full blast, like those in Manchuria. The big blackboards hung up on the walls were mute witnesses to the daily production level attained by each "work unit." The newly liberated women and the children also took part in the work. Foremen wore striped jackets and carried a handful of pens and pencils in their breast pockets. Technicians became specially privileged Citizens of Honor and the Russians rode around in closed cars; every so often the rumor spread that before long all that activity was going to give China the key to atomic energy, that awesome energy that had fallen from the sky like rain and prostrated China's proud and hated neighbor, Japan.

Chou En-lai contemplated this spectacle and observed: "The Christians trust in God. The humanists trust in man's capacity. We Marxists trust in the products of nature and in the economical use one makes of them."

How many workers and small producers were there spread across China? Not even Mao's census could tell for sure. The human working conditions were fantastic; usually, a worker was stripped to the waist and wore rubber-soled slippers or the traditional sandals. In many cases the workers had to use the most rudimentary means of transport, such as the classic pole across the shoulders with a basket or bucket dangling from each end, surrounded by the maddening racket of steam engines, pneumatic drills, and cranes. They bravely faced the elements and never ceased singing hymns to Mao. All over the nation, even in desert areas, the Chinese people were producing sources of wealth. The object was always the same: to make the Great Leap Forward a reality, imitate the Soviet Union's progress, and then overtake and finally surpass the production of the imperialistic West.

While it is true that the individual's efforts and importance scarcely counted at all, a man being important only as one more statistic, a "work unit," it is nevertheless also true that many people sacrificed themselves voluntarily: industrialization was so wonderful! Even the physical senses were delighted and stimulated: the shiny new machines were so smooth to the touch, the lubricants smelled so nice, and the steady hum of the conveyor belts was so pleasant, as was the roar of the locomotives. In short, everything seemed to bear out the slogan: "A few years of effort and a thousand years of happiness."

Hand in hand with the industrialization drive the state undertook an ambitious reforestation program; Mao blamed the wastefulness of the ancient tree-felling policy of China for a good portion of the calamities of nature which the nation suffered. The program seemed encouraging, especially since among the specialists that Russia sent were many scientists who had worked for years with reforestation in the Arctic, attempting to moderate the climate. Millions of trees were now planted, beginning with the Gobi Desert region, in an effort to break the freezing winds that swept down from Siberia. The initial results were splendid and enabled foreign observers to be shown how the hills alongside the rivers and streams were turning green for the first time in centuries. Populars and acacias were planted beside the dusty highways, frequently in rows of four. "These millions of trees," explained Party leaders, "will help to avoid erosion, thus saving the soil and conserving the rainfall; later on they will supply us with the wood so badly needed for building."

Mao made Marx's famous idea his own: "Until now, philosophers have only interpreted the world; now, it is our turn to *transform* it." Mao proposed to transform the entire face of China. He was turning the workers into theorists, the land into trees and the farm girls into Party teachers. He conceded such importance to the reforestation program that people began to call him "the man of the forests." Mao only smiled; he did not mind in the least. In his poems he had spoken with devotion of the trunks and leaves of the trees and the mysterious way in which they multiplied in response to some inner stirring. But the success of his reforestation drive depended on doing away with the parasites that infected China, so he inaugurated a campaign against the four principle plagues: flies, mosquitoes, rats, and sparrows. "If every Chinese kills one fly a day, seven hundred million flies will die every day," he pointed out. The extermination of rats was spectacular. The method used to kill sparrows was that of simple fatigue: pots and pans or other kitchen utensils were banged with spoons and ladles until the concert drove the sparrows mad and they dropped exhausted to the ground, where they were mercilessly killed.

The moment for playing his trump card finally arrived; Mao was at last going to launch the agrarian reform. What a resounding battle cry: Agrarian Reform! It was a struggle to the death with the big landowners and feudal barons. Five hundred million Chinese were awaiting the outcome, the practical results of the operation. By no means was it an easy task. In ancient times various Chinese emperors had tried from time to time to carry out a distribution of parcels of land, but afterwards they simply abandoned the peasants to their ignorance and empiricism and the land soon proved how cruel it could be, denying them a decent or even meagre living. At other times, the farm workers became no more than mere accessories of the land they worked, without the slightest hope of ever owning it; at times like that, a drought or epidemic was enough to finish them off. The same mistakes could not be repeated now.

Mao, who as usual was preparing to carry out this latest project from an objective point of view, wanted to make very clear the goals he was aiming at, so that no one would be likely to fool himself. Liu Chao-chi was given the job of setting forth the doctrine: "The purpose of agrarian reform is not to give land to the poor peasants nor to relieve their suffering. This would be an ideal for philanthropists but not for Marxists. The agrarian reform's goal is the freeing of the nation's agricultural strength by means of the complete *suppression* of the landed class, the *suppression* of the rich farmers." So that there would be no doubts on this subject, another Party chief stated: "If the peasants are not permitted to beat and kill the landowners, it will be difficult to mobilize them. And without doing this, it will be useless to try to eliminate a thousand years of feudal exploitation."

As a matter of fact, the execution of the landowners had begun right after the proclamation of the Chinese People's Republic, with the ex-tenants in the front row watching, but a certain disorganization and confusion has complicated the program. Now it was to be carried out systematically, cohesively.

The method of operation selected was efficiency itself. A "Purification Commission" arrived in a town and immediately called a meeting of the peasants and listened to their complaints. These sessions were called "expressions of bitterness." The peasants dug up and brought to light a long series of injustices, thanks to which their dreams of bettering their lot had been frustrated. The guilty parties, sometimes charged with offenses committed as long as twenty years earlier, were summoned and tried without losing time, after which their goods were confiscated and distributed. It was not unusual for the poorer farmers to inform on one another because of some minor grievance or in order to fatten the collective booty. The punishment was something to behold; the village elders watched the ceremony with an emotion akin to astonishment.

These "trials," presided over by the People's Courts—the bodies charged with applying the law were called "Courts of Justice"—reached the limit of their cruelty with the repressive campaign of 1951, which swept across China like a cataclysm. The persecution was horrible. Many bodies were strung up in trees and others rolled out into ditches from the backs of trucks. It is impossible to say just how many people were killed. The arrival of these "Purification Commissions" touched off scenes of stark terror in the towns. Many landowning farmers chose to commit suicide rather than face the unbending party representatives. Finally, in view of the way it was spreading, suicide was officially declared "an illegal act against the state."

The method of land distribution that Mao proposed was all-out collectivization; he had apparently learned nothing from the Soviet Union's failures in this respect.

With this campaign, the entire panorama of the countryside, literally the whole rural picture, began to change. New forms and shapes never before seen in China invaded the country roads and replaced the miserable familiar sights that had lasted for thousands of years. Carts with rubber tires appeared, new ploughs with shiny metal shares, irrigation pumps, tractors, harvesters, combines, chemical fertilizers. The peasants gave expression to their joy by rolling like cats in the hay stacks and alfalfa piles, and like Mao, letting themselves get soaked in the rain. In addition, teams of experts gave them classes in deep ploughing, utilization of streams and seed selection, prevention of local diseases in livestock, etc. Furthermore, in extensive regions like Sinkiang millions of acres were turned over to the raising of cotton, and deserts such as the Takla Makan were to be converted into fertile plains like those in Canada. The crash program for utilization of all arable land became such an obsession that Mao conceived of a campaign aimed against cemeteries! The cemeteries would have to be done away with; the land in them was so rich they could be turned into vegetable gardens. At the same time, the farmers were to be taught to mix the pulverized bones with other synthetic foods in a series of nutrition and fertilization experiments. The peasants recoiled in anguish; China had always venerated ancestors. Omar Khayyam's phrase came true: "Who knows if the lump turned up and trodden was the tornout eye of some handsome youth?" But the Chinese wept and gnashed their teeth. The owner of the harvests was, of course, the state; she also fixed prices. Mao was unalterable. His right-hand man, Liu Chao-chi, had spoken clearly: thinking of the immediate welfare of the farm workers would be an ideal for philanthropists but not for Marxists.

However, the agrarian reform did not stop at this point. Its nucleus, its reason for being, its very essence was the establishment of the People's Communes. Mao decided to impose on a huge scale the tiny experiment he had carried out in Yenan at the end of The Long March. The People's Communes would constitute perhaps the riskiest venture ever undertaken by man on earth, since it proposed nothing less than the destruction of the concept of family life, the radical extermination of the complexes created by the living together of several members of the same blood.

Unfortunately, Mao's project had to be postponed. The year was 1953. Mao would later call it "the year of catastrophes." First, Stalin died. Next, Nature herself seemed to react against the plans drawn up in Peking's Summer Palace. The rivers, created by the tears of the mythical giant Pank-Ou, who lived for eighteen thousand years, overflowed their banks. Floods, frosts, typhoid, and hunger followed in quick succession.

Mao considered Stalin's death a national disaster. He had been Mao's teacher, his "elder brother." He had taught him the triology of power: the army, the police and the courts, as well as the organization and executive administration of the Party. Stalin, throughout his long career as revolutionary leader, had always considered compassion and pity to be bourgeois sentiments; this delighted Mao, since his personal disposition led him toward the same conclusion. Stalin—the tough, introverted ex-seminarian, terror

personified, hated by Trotsky and called "inhuman" by
Tito—Stalin had died. Mao would weep bitterly for his
loss now, and at the first chance he got would hurry to pay
homage to the mummified corpse, laid next to that of Lenin.

One had to go back a long way to find anything similar
to the terrible natural calamities that struck China that
year. Once again the Hwang Ho became China's "Great
Sorrow." It swept away all the hydroelectric plants, factories, and homemade furnaces in its path; it would be
necessary to start all over again. In the North, the freezing
temperatures had frozen the wheat, barley, and corn; in
the South, the rice was lost. The Chinese People's Republic
had not been able to avoid the catastrophe and consequently could not escape the famine either.

Once the delay enforced on him was over—it was well
into 1954 by this time—Mao was at last able to go ahead
with his plans for the People's Communes. The operation
began in the villages, following the already tested formula:
community work, organized militarily and directed with
trumpet or whistle blasts, a thirteen-hour work day, nightly
indoctrination sessions, meals in the canteen, the babies in
the nursery and the old people in the "Houses of Happiness." Men and women slept separately, each in an allotted
space of slightly over ten square feet; for husbands and
wives the Communes set up periodical "encounters" similar
to the "conjugal Thursdays" organized in some Mexican
prisons. Nothing belonged to anyone, there was no such
thing as savings, everything was collective, from the closets
to the latrines and soap. There was a weekly weight check,
sensible organization of spare time and vacations, and even
collective visits to watch the executions. In the event a
friendship grew up between two members of a Commune,
the Party delegate was empowered to approve it or to

transfer one of the two to some far-off post. In case of sickness, visits were strictly limited to the hours prescribed. In case of death, a truck carried the body off to some unknown destination. Radio sets, which were community property, could only be listened to at the Party delegate's suggestion. The press was, of course, government controlled and the small amount of mail which did circulate—a great many of the peasants were illiterate—was delayed because of censorship. The inspectors carried out exhaustive weekly questioning sessions and then filled in endless data sheets on the progress of each "work unit." These inspectors might suddenly approach any member of the Commune and demand: "What were you just thinking about?" They were also known to separate two people on the spur of the moment and force each to describe the subject of the conversation that had been interrupted.

A bare nutritional minimum was distributed in the canteen and blue cotton uniforms and rubber or felt boots were also supplied to all the members of the Communes. Still, living conditions became hateful. The individual began to doubt his own existence; nevertheless, how was one to get together with one's spouse, or brothers and sisters, or parents or children? Members of the same family might be living together in the same Commune but their communication was agonizing, since they realized the impossibility of loving one another. Not only had they been uprooted from their homes and carried off to antiseptic new collective "homes," but the whistle was forever cutting short their conversations and even the furtive glances they exchanged. Little by little people began to develop cleverly concocted codes; a whole new metaphorical language came into being, with double meanings and mimicry or song as its means of expression. The Party delegates frowned but there was little

they could do about it. The children cared for in the collective nurseries were frequently transferred without warning. For "reasons of hygiene" or supposed shortages in supplies the children were moved to another nursery in some distant province; the real reason was the confessed ideal that children should grow up ". . . tall, independent, and agile, without any other desire than that of working and thus making China great."

The classic passive resistance of the Chinese peasant began and Mao was told about it. His reply was a quotation from the Czech revolutionary leader Zapotocky: "The philanthropic, liberal, and incorrect idea that the main thing is to help and sustain the individual is very widespread. What kind of Socialist viewpoint is this? The only thing necessary is to protect production. The harm that might be done to a worker's way of life is not so important as the harm done to production."

However, Mao was a subtle and clever man, a man with a third eye in the middle of his forehead, and he eventually began to re-evaluate the Communes. At one point he had serious doubts about them. He realized that performing laboratory experiments in Yenan caves was not the same as applying the Commune method to all of China. He also understood that there were natural laws at work in the world which were difficult to defy. At the last moment, though, he cast aside his doubts, in spite of the warning of Russia, the "elder brother." He went on pushing his Communes, "precisely because they failed in Russia." He even carried the idea into the cities, where the results were worse yet. The industrial workers put up an even greater resistance, since they had been accustomed to greater incentive and stimuli.

The progress of the Communes was a slow and painful pilgrimage. Modifications in form were attempted but the result was always the same. The peasants preferred the uncertainty of former times; although they had been miserable, at least they had had their own homes, a chance to embrace their loved ones and possess some odds and ends of their own. "Let us return to our bamboo huts," they begged. Mao gave them instead long speeches, which they answered with tears.

* * *

"Why do you have so many children?"
"Because we must wage war."
"But why must you wage war?"
"Because we have too many children!"

This joke originated in Shanghai and quickly spread across the country. It aptly caricatured Mao's circular argument regarding the birth-rate problem.

Without a doubt, a wave of ill humor had swept over Peking, the city of nameless streets. In the very midst of the Commune period his technicians confronted Mao with an old and troublesome problem: since 1949, the year that the Party came into power, the population of China had increased by over one hundred million souls. If the same rate kept up, an increase of about fifteen million per year, any increased production would be of no value to the nation; there would simply be more mouths to consume the added production.

Mao put aside for the moment the incessant improvements he had talked of in his book of poems, *Of Stones and the Wind*. Indeed, he and Chou En-lai had repeatedly spoken of the possibility that China would one day have a billion inhabitants, but the problem was rapidly assuming alarming proportions. Mao disappeared for a couple of weeks, going to a hidden retreat where he spent the time relaxing and killing flies with a little bamboo swatter, thinking all the while. At the end of his holiday, after conferring with his Minister of Public Health, Li Teh-chuan, he announced the beginning of a birth control campaign. It was apparently hard for him to bring himself to make this decision, which affected the very roots of life itself. His explanation was unimpassioned and objective, as always: "If we succeed in lowering the birth rate, our standard of living will rise more quickly. For this reason we must establish throughout China an adequate means of birth control."

This campaign was more incisive than any of the preceding ones. Marx and Malthus strolled arm in arm through all the Chinese villages. Tons of brochures and informational material were printed and hygiene courses were begun everywhere. The mechanics of reproduction and fertilization were painstakingly explained and illustrated by means of graphs and charts. The word "abortion" was foremost in everyone's mind. In hospitals and mobile clinics, teams of nurses instructed people in the art of aborting, the use of ovules, suppositories, and medicinal herbs mixed according to ancient Chinese traditions. In the cities, eighteen-year-old girls gave the necessary explanations, pointer in hand before their charts. Contraceptives, which were being mass produced, dropped in price to almost nothing.

It was a long and hard fight with all shades and variations of reactions. The means of coercion set up were so effective that part of the population obeyed, but the idea of large families was so deeply rooted that there was a series of complex domestics dramas all over China; there were many cases of divorce or separation, with each party denying his or her share of the blame, and many mothers committed suicide. Also, everyone still remembered the wide publicity previously given to the Russian system of painless childbirth; now this new policy seemed so contradictory. And then too, since 1949, really militant Communists had cherished the idea of offering Mao's China thousands of sons who would later rule the country.

Infanticides, above all in homes where twins were born, became so widespread that the new Nuptial Law drawn up by the government declared in Article 13: "It is absolutely forbidden to kill newly born babies or perpetrate similar crimes." The "similar crimes" referred to were abandoning children in the country or at the collective nurseries, or exposing them to fatal diseases.

In short, the Chinese character presented an active resistance to the birth control campaign announced by Mao Tse-tung. Once more, the women said "No," and although Mao cleverly managed to salvage the situation by a dialectical revision, it was clear that the Party had had to do an abrupt about-face.

In Shanghai and all across China people continued to smile at the sarcastic riddle:

"Why do you have so many children?"
"Because we must wage war."
"But why must you wage war?"
"Because we have too many children."

Some Western observers, anti-Communists, saw in these failures a sign of decomposition. "Mao wanted to go further than Russia and has run up against cold facts. The Marxist experiment in China was exciting but short."

What hopeless myopia! Mao's failures were like raindrops in the ocean. The Party was quite prepared to change its line completely, exchanging one set of principles for its opposite, and not a single loyal Party member would so much as blush. As for the opposition, which witnessed with horror the sequence of experiments carried out on human beings, no comment was forthcoming. The forces of repression condemned all opposition to silence, usually with a bullet in the nape of the neck. Nor did the three and a half million Christians in China have the slightest chance to make their voices heard. The Party bore down so on this religious minority, basing its campaign on spectacular lies, that the Sacred Heart Home in Nanking, to cite one example, was accused of murdering babies and became known as "Little Buchenwald."

Now that the birth control campaign had come to a halt, Mao, still determined to put into practice another of the experiments rehearsed in Yenan at the end of The Long March, undertook the preparation of the Kun-Pa, the leadership teams chosen from among the most promising young people.

These "leadership teams," which actually already existed throughout the Marxist world, from Rumania and East Germany to the jungles of Malaya and North Korea, were to be to the Chinese Revolution what the Hwang Ho, the Yellow River, was to the nation's agriculture and new industry: the backbone, the formative and indispensable ingredient. On it might depend the very success of the Marxist creed itself, the final mutation that Mao had envisioned from Socialism to Communism.

The "Pioneer Youth" had already been subjected to an exhaustive indoctrination, a ceaseless bombardment of Mao's doctrine regarding love and hate. Every Chinese youngster had to have five loves: the Motherland, the People, Work, Science, and Public Property; he was to have but two hates: the religions, all of which were reactionary, and American imperialism.

Now it was the young people's turn. In Yenan the "young elite" had been isolated and obliged to practice self-criticism and mutual denunciation. Now, all over China, even more was attempted. The self-criticism was aimed not only at actions but at intentions as well and would cover the period from the age of reason up to the boy's entry into the Kun-Pa. It was necessary for the catechumen to spread out the whole picture of his life before him in order to inform the Party what had been his severest emotional blow as a child, why he had begun to smoke, why he had begun to drink, why he had loved his parents. . . . Futhermore, the candidate had to confess out loud and publicly all his errors, in order to develop the required sense of guilt; this confession had to be made cold-bloodedly, without hesitation or stuttering, "as though speaking of someone else altogether," under pain of being accused of disloyalty, of blocking the "purification process" that the Kun-Pas were carrying out.

The law was identical regarding mutual accusation. One had to keep in mind constantly that one of the main objectives of the Kun-Pas was "to attain a spirit of espionage and a thorough knowledge of its most efficient techniques." Consequently, it was necessary to watch one's friends closely and later inform on them; any scruples on the subject were irrelevant. Careful observation sharpened the critical sense and provided useful bits of evidence. Needless to say, there was no truth outside the Party and it would have been ridiculous and indeed presumptuous to put one's personal judgement ahead of a doctrine which, in slightly less than forty years, had transformed society.

The free world has been able to gather certain very concrete facts about the first Kun-Pa training seminars. The majority of the students chosen were between eighteen and twenty-four years old. The "apprenticeship," which lasted about nine months, was carried out in a camp; upon entering, all bonds with relatives and even old friends were severed. This breaking off with the old was called "cutting the pigtail." The pupils in these training camps could leave them only for "excursions to the countryside," closely supervised of course; such "excursions" usually consisted in watching executions or sometimes visiting public-works projects underway. The plan of physical and mental exertion drawn up for the trainees kept them constantly on the go, with practically no time for distraction. Uncertainty was one of the basic factors in the educational program. The future leader never knew whether his behavior was correct or whether the Party delegate was going to denounce him in front of all the other students. Human reactions common in man, like tears or humor, were forbidden in the Kun-Pa since they were considered bourgeois values befitting a society which one was constantly obliged to refer to in nothing but scornful terms. The whole thing was in fact a psychological plan designed to create beings with automatic reflexes. "Whatever is against Mao is well on its way to failure." Mao's Revolution demanded "new men," just as once upon a time the religious had demanded them, except that they had promised personal happiness in a transcendental hereafter and Marxism proposed to achieve a collective happiness in an immediate here and now.

The two philosophical principles which guided the Kun-Pa teaching were: "Any emotion or affection is subversive," and "All lives are public property."

The Maoist man was forbidden to display emotion and to love. Men had to be as hard as the stones used in the Great Wall of China. Any emotion implied weakness, a dangerous inclination of the spirit to work against what logic advised. A Chinese Communist ought not to give way to any emotion, since the adverse world, the world still unredeemed, required him to be constantly on his guard. The history of the bourgeoisie was filled with frivolous and corrosive acts performed in the name of some sentiment connected with love. The leadership corps, the young rulers of tomorrow, were not even supposed to love the Party. One had to serve the Party even though at some given moment one might hate it. What mattered and counted was not personal opinion, nor transitory feelings, but only the final result. "Dogma is less useful than fertilizer."

Everything boiled down to the fact that life was public property. The individual as such had no importance and no worth. The individual only had importance insofar as he constituted a fraction of the group, and consequently it was licit to sacrifice an unlimited number of individuals if it brought about some good for the Kun-Pa, for the community. For the individual to be content was valid if it brought happiness to everyone else; it was quite out of order to be sad for personal reasons. The older Chinese called the dead "Guests of the Highest," because they supposed that somehow, somewhere they were still alive, but the Maoists believed in nothing but the Earth, and that on Earth nothing belonged to the person and that the person belonged to everyone. The Kun-Pa system was superior to Confucius because Confucius taught filial piety, cornerstone of selfishness and servitude. Kun-Pa was superior to Lao-tse because Lao-tse taught an abstract formula of sanctity, the nucleus of superstition and dependence. Kun-Pa was superior to Buddha because Buddha remained ecstatic even in the face of evil, and it was superior to Christ because He taught turning the other cheek. Kun-Pa, in short, led back to the fertile origins of Marxism, which required the ideal fusion of all lives in one, understanding "life" to mean the material body and its higher product, thought.

The training courses undertaken by Mao in China gave much better results than those attempted in Russia and ran into less resistance. In fact, they were a heartening success. The young people chosen very soon renounced their egos and scarcely hesitated at all when the time came to renounce their friends; not even the person exposed was particularly horrified by his betrayal. Anyone who refrained from publicly exposing his fellow students left himself wide open to reprisals. Failure to inform on someone who had erred was considered as serious as failure to confess voluntarily one's guilt in case of temptation to homosexuality. In both cases, the punishment was invariably radical. The accused simply disappeared from the training camp and for days all sorts of rumors about his fate circulated secretly; he was usually assigned to a forced-labor brigade.

The Kun-Pa instructors had selected as their theme song an anthem published in *Pravda* on May 21, 1934; its composer was a Russian woman named Pronia Kolibin, and it stated in part:

> You are a cruel saboteur, Mother,
> Working against the kolkhoz.
> You are my sworn enemy,
> And since you do not love the kolkhoz,
> I must do away with your contemptible life.

The Chinese Communist Party nourished itself—and continues to nourish itself—on the leader squads trained in the Kun-Pas. The Party could depend on them without reservation. Their dialectic was consistently solid, especially when the listeners were farm workers. Furthermore, a good measure of their strength rested upon their integrity, their example. These corps were above bribery and corruption, and enjoyed as much fame as had the highly disciplined "Red Dragons" in their day.

Mao, who had just announced the second five-year plan, was so pleased with the news of the spectacular success of the Kun-Pa system that he decided to extend it through the "Rectification Campaign." Liu Chao-chi was the official delegated with the responsibility for this tremendous undertaking. "From here on," he announced, "the rectification campaign will be adopted as the official means of ideological reform . . . . in every company and office, in all military units, in rural areas, in schools, etc. everyone will analyze his past life and perform the proper public confession, with a promise to amend his deeds." This operation was known as "tatsepao," or "striking one's breast." The block committees set up to administer the operation were overwhelmed with applications. There were some who felt like "new men" upon completing their "tatsepao"; on the other hand, there were some who fell into profound confusion. The experience was especially complex in the case of the intellectuals, some of whom went so far as to repeat the process four and five times. Lian Sau Chᶜeng, the foremost architect in China, confessed that his two main sins had been "aspiring to have a house of his own" and "having done everything possible so that his father, the reformer Chᶜi Ch-ao, would be proud of him." Hsia-ai-ju, professor of geography, confessed his fondness for English professional publications in his field. Kentin Iᶜan, a top sociologist, admitted that in spite of his efforts he "could not bring himself to hate America with the necessary vehemence." Athletes and sports figures also underwent their own "tatsepao." They accused themselves of not having won enough laurel wreathes, prizes, and gold medals for the Homeland,

and of having been more zealous for bodily fitness than for the prestige of China. Among other crimes and errors confessed were ". . . greater interest in one's profession than in the Revolution" and ". . . having thought oneself worthy to be a disciple of Mao Tse-tung."

This rectification campaign, whose forerunner had been the ideological reform movement undertaken in 1953, the year Stalin died, was backed up by the motion pictures shown—never was there a kiss on the screen—and by the stage and puppet plays. The plots of every dramatic art-form were a systematic hymn to the prodigal son, the repentant sinner. Any story, song, or script which did not extol the glory of The Long March, the efforts of some village or other to turn itself into a People's Commune, the Battle of Sankunryung, etc. was sure to bring down official wrath upon its author's head, forcing him to repent publicly under pain of being sent to the factories or the mines, his works branded as "poisonous weeds."

But the really practical manifestation of the rectification program was the illiteracy drive, aimed against a plague much more widespread in China than the forest sparrows or ancestor worship. "To be illiterate is to plot against the greatness of China," the peasants were informed. It was a hard fight, since the written Chinese language is ideographic and not phonetic. In many villages, besides the classes given by the sole teacher, the Party delegate, people began to use the whitewashed walls as practice space for their newly acquired writing skill. The students were urged to write their first phrases on them, and the peasants began to fill the great white expanses with confessions, pictures, and even poems, to the point where the newspapers started talking of a new mural art.

From the first phase—the application of the rectification campaign to illiteracy—the Party passed on to general education, which from the very start had been directed toward the formation of specialists and militant politicians rather than "men" in the humanistic Western sense. Official policy on the subject was outspoken: "Public instruction must be at the service of the proletariat and controlled and directed by the Party. Teaching must be anti-imperialistic, Marxist-Leninist; it must destroy the vestiges of American influence and propagate the spirit and viewpoint of the people." Elsewhere it was stated that: "One must be both expert and Red."

Naturally, the rectification process stimulated scientific and technical formation much more than literary, juridical, or artistic formation. One theoretician—Mao Tse-tung—was enough. "The scientist who collaborates in the study of cell growth or the technician who turns out a good optical instrument is more useful to China than a good artist or a mere admirer of beauty, à la Lao-tse."

Speaking once about the machinery set in motion by Stalin, Trotsky called it a "hitherto unseen weapon of submission." Tito, speaking of the machinery set in motion by Mao Tse-tung, declared: "Not even Stalin was so inhuman."

Tito's statement is perhaps the most adequate commentary which Mao's psychological strategy in China can inspire. Mao has probably gone beyond all limits of impunity known to date, and the result has been one enormous grief. All the information on China received from the most diverse sources, giving what may be considered a representative cross section of opinion, indicates that a tremendous gloom hangs over all of the nation, except perhaps for certain sectors of the youth; there is a significant percentage of cases of melancholy and madness, to the point where many of the confiscated Buddhist monasteries have been turned into insane asylums.

Needless to say Mao's procedures would be tolerated nowhere else, not even in Russia. One of the many things which he has made his own is this statement by Lasalle: "The people don't realize how unhappy they really are; we shall show them." Mao has proceeded little by little to enmesh the ordinary citizen in a web of stifling ideas, always the same, in line with one of the basic maxims of his government: "In reality, what the Chinese people want is a state which will take care of everything for them, to relieve them of even thinking for themselves." This maxim is based on the historical action of the farmers at the time of the late Roman Empire who, having been freed from servitude, preferred to voluntarily turn themselves and their lands over to the nearest lord in return for his protection.

Mao has achieved undeniable progress. He seems to have eliminated the great famines, although recently the old specter has been rearing its head once more. He has reduced the seriousness of the floods and practically wiped out plagues. He has lowered infant mortality, has discovered important mineral deposits, and has obviously exercised an absolute, constant control over the masses. At the same time, he has carried out spectacular public-works projects and has started the nation on the road to industrialization, especially with regard to nuclear energy and steel.

Consequently, Mao claims he is satisfied and that the foundation for a definitive emancipation has been laid. However, his optimism has not been shared even by all of his collaborators, some of whom accuse him of personalism, of wanting to skip over intermediate stages, of defending a program which ignores the sufferings of the people. Western observers, who are motivated by a set of values incompatible with Marxism, feel that too flagrant a disproportion exists between the advances Mao has achieved and the price they have cost, between the improvements he has been able to bring about and the toll China has had to pay.

All-out nationalism, hatred for the West, a mystique of work, the blossoming forth of factories, reforestation, the agrarian reform, the People's Communes, the Kun-Pa system, the rectification campaign, etc., are all concrete examples of the methods employed by Mao Tse-tung since 1949. All of them together have produced a seismic upheaval in the body and soul of China, but they have not brought about peace of mind, not to mention happiness, nor have they laid the foundations for the eventual attainment of such peace and happiness.

Since 1949, which is to say during almost fifteen long years of rule, Mao has sacrificed millions of lives, precious lives loved by someone; the Chinese Communist Party has never tried to conceal the enormous number of executions. Various frontier territories have been annexed and entire populations of people have been transplanted to the interior. Mao has burned practically all the visible, ancient patrimony of China, from the secular quarters of Peking to the vast archives of classical poetry. He has set about destroying the family unit and has even turned the trees into propaganda billboards. After almost fifteen years of this unhuman revolution, surrounded by all the standard totalitarian and repressive measures, purged of capitalistic scruples and alienated from the world of emotions, the Chinese have not only seen themselves stripped of every last vestige of liberty, man's most precious gift, but have continued to suffer a level of life far inferior to that of any, even the poorest, Western nation. While it is true that China's problems, given her geographic density, are infinitely more complex than those of Sweden or Paraguay, on the other hand her resources are infinitely greater.

Mao has achieved startling advances in the over-all picture; it would be a gross mistake to claim the contrary. But up to now neither the Chinaman's body nor his soul has profited by these advances.

The Chinaman was formerly ironical; he now disguises his irony. The Chinaman, with his poetic insight, once converted the real and concrete into abstraction; he now does just the opposite, turning abstractions into something as tangible as a crane or a tractor. The Chinaman formerly loved; he loved his ancestors, the trade he practiced, the hereditary forms of his culture. Now he lives perpetually pursued by hatred. He has to hate this, that, and the other thing; he must hate his bourgeois neighbor, the cloud too heavily laden with rain, the United States, incurable diseases, morality based upon custom, religion. . . . The Chinaman formerly lied to prove his cleverness, because he got a delicious intellectual thrill out of it; now he lies to defend himself or to denounce his companions.

On the physical plane, with reference to obtaining the necessities, Tibor Mende has stated in a penetrating article:

In the present-day Chinese home there are nothing but utensils and practical, mass-produced items, although there are more of them than in Russia during the first two five-year plans that Stalin masterminded. If the average Chinese permits himself only a few luxuries like going to a movie once in a great while, buying a fountain pen—a mediocre imitation of the Parker 51—or a few books and a pack of cigarettes, he may perhaps have a little money left over. In this case, the state shops and department stores offer him a surprising assortment of articles, including radios, record players, cameras, bicycles, etc., all made in China. But since the price of these articles frequently represents several months' wages for a skilled worker, the Chinese working-class man usually has to content himself with a small mechanical toy, a record, or a chocolate bar.

This is true only in the cities and industrial zones; in the rural areas, thanks to the failure of the agrarian reform and collectivization, scarcity is considerably more acute, above all in the mountain regions.

4

---◆---

COMMUNISM AND THE WEST

It is clear that Mao's debut was made possible by unjust social conditions, just as was Lenin's. In a fair and equitable society, Mao's ravings would not have been possible. At the outset of the struggle in 1921, the Chinese leader could have papered all the walls of the Summer Palace in Peking with cartoons depicting the shameful deeds committed by the officials of his country's government. In the social order of those days there existed all over the world a discord similar to that which currently exists between machines and human emotions. The word "masses" had no meaning, nor did even the word "people." Work was not a highly prized commodity. The tenor of the times seemed to proclaim "Up with rights, down with duties." Such a situation cried out to heaven but heaven was covered over with heavy clouds—perverse human desires—and the result was rebellion, a vast enslaving rebellion reminiscent of the floods of the Yellow River.

Right on the Asiatic continent itself there were some men like Ghandi, believers in "satyagraha," non-violent resistance. But the general rule was aggressive reaction. There were others who believed in timid protests, in "expressions of bitterness"; they were condemned to failure. The powerful continued to oppress the weak.

It was inevitable that the impetus of various inventions and technical progress should have given rise to Hegel, Marx, Engels, Lenin, and Stalin, all of whom leaned heavily upon Darwin's theory of evolution, which they in turn applied to the class struggle. It was inevitable that a Mao Tsetung should also appear in Asia. The tremendous responsibility of capitalism has been that it has lacked the spiritual quality and the political sense required to make popular rebellion unnecessary. It slumbered along so peacefully in its bed of roses and banknotes that, had it not been for the brutal and primitive challenge of a few minds, it would probably still be roaming loose around the world, shouting insults with impunity and giving orders to all the poor and humble as though they belonged to some inferior race. Centuries of domination had failed to innoculate the capitalists with the glorious serum of brotherhood among men, a brotherhood preached by Christianity and perfectly compatible with a diversity of talents, efforts, and even the whims of misfortune.

The results are plain enough. The rebellion, which began with the French Revolution, has culminated with the hydrogen bomb in the hands of the Communists, as well as with their domination of half the earth and their serious and ever-growing threat to the other half.

This rebellion, logical and inexorable, brought on by the waste and monopoly of capitalism and the privileges of the pith-helmet class, backed up by rifles, has its other face too, just like the moon. In fact, the remedy chosen by this rebellion's promoters turns out to be spectacular but inoperative, since in a basic way it does not manage to solve any of the injustices inherent in capitalism, or the problems created by capitalism's actions. In the Marxist doctrine the only thing that is different about power is that it changes hands. Communism was born as a protest against the dictatorship of the individual but has fallen into the dictatorship of the collectivity. What is more, in the Communist regime the masses wind up deifying not only the collectivity and its epitome, which is the state, but in addition they deify an individual, the leader who carried them to victory, and transform him into a master much more despotic than any who preceded him. Consequently these masses, far from improving their status and coming of age, become slaves twice over, a situation which has its supreme example in China. Marx, for his part, foresaw this when he said: "Liberty is a delicate mechanism, suitable only for adults." So far as the rest goes, Communism carries its internal contradiction to its furthest extreme and, while considering religious mysticism, belief in a Supreme Being, and the ardent desire to incorporate oneself into this Being as malignant for the people, nevertheless converts its followers into mystics as fanatical as any militant Christians or Buddhists, leads them into raptures and trances, and instills them with the double desire of offering their lives for the Party and of incorporating themselves one day into the supreme goal, which is the triumph of the universal proletariat.

Undoubtedly, Communism's great victory consists in having distinguished the social significance of several important words—"people," "worker," etc.—and in having created in the wealthy and powerful classes a feeling of guilt, obliging them, with full justice, to give up a part of their showy privileges. But the great failure of Communism consists in not having created a socio-political structure to repair the the errors of capitalism, to build a body of positive doctrine over the corpse of capitalism. Communism has been the great prosecuting attorney of this era; nothing less but nothing more either.

Now the question is: "Who will stop this prosecuting attorney's bloody harangue?" The optimists, who abound in the West, speak of the "progressively bourgeois tendencies" in Russia and the great "absorptive capacity" of China. "Russia will evolve by itself," they tell us, "it is already undergoing an evolution. And as for China, its philosophical personality is such that Communism will sink and be lost in it, being finally absorbed." Both statements are not only yet to be demonstrated, not only still hypothetical, but in the concrete case of China it is presumable that if such an absorption took place it would by no means signal the weakening of the Marxist malignancy but quite the contrary. As a matter of fact, it is possible that Marxism might add to its own natural aggressiveness some of the artistic but lethal subtleties on which the hangmen of the Celestial Empire have always prided themselves.

Confucius once told his minister Pe: "I have known that in the nations of the West a holy man will be born who will put an end to disorders without exercising any sort of government; without speaking, he will inspire a spontaneous faith; without provoking disturbances, he will perform a sea of actions; nobody can say his name, but I have heard that he will be the true Saint."

One would say that this is a prophecy about the coming of Jesus, but why did Confucius dictate it to his minister Pe? His words vividly recall those of John the Baptist.

There is no indication that Mao is familiar with these words of Confucius although he may very well be, since when he was younger he was assistant librarian at the University of Peking. But there is proof that he has dedicated some time and attention to the two-thousand-year-old phenomenon called Christianity, a phenomenon which is scarcely a prime factor in China itself—the three and a half million Christians there are condemned to silence—but which counts in a special way in the vast regions of the West whose way of life Mao wishes to destroy.

On this point as on others perhaps less important, Mao differs from Lenin. In spite of Marx's unequivocable position on the subject, Lenin gave little importance to the religious phenomenon. In Lenin's opinion religion was a circumstantial defensive reaction which would die by itself of inertia as soon as the masses liberated themselves from capitalist oppression. For Lenin, the religious problem was a "third class" one (how different was Stalin's attitude!), and if Communism ought to persecute religion it was not because of its importance but rather because of its ties to capitalism. "By persecuting religion we speed up the bankruptcy of capitalism.".

Mao has shown himself to be more combative. Not only has he excluded God from his revolutionary credo, adopting as a substitute the materialistic interpretation of history, but he also considers Christianity as the only dike which could contain the "prosecutor's bloody harangue," the expansion of enslaving Marxism. He has a sound basis for this idea inasmuch as Christianity is the only doctrine, other than Marxism, which involves and commits the entire being, the being as an individual and as a member of the group.

His preoccupation with Christianity dates back some time, to the days when he directed the Communist newspaper in Shanghai. At that time he wrote: "We have to confess that before the Bolshevik Revolution of 1917 the only economically developed countries in the world were those guided by Christianity; the rest continued oppressed by hunger, misery, and the superstitions of remote ages." He also wrote: "Christianity is on the side of the imperialistic exploiters. Nevertheless, it permits a scientific, technical, and economic development which, although inferior to that which could be reached by a Communist society, should by no means be underestimated." And then too, as we have mentioned, Christianity has existed for almost two thousand years; for Mao, the product of an Asiatic culture, the age, the antiquity, the *time* of things has always been an important determining factor in measuring their potentiality.

Mao calls this "living according to realities and not according to the abstractions of Lao-tse." For this reason, while congratulating himself on the fact that Christianity means hardly anything in China, he is conscious of its implicit power in the non-Asiatic world he intends to conquer. He is conscious of its implicit power even in Russia itself, and has heard rumors of a vigorous religious reaction, perceptible above all since Stalin's death; this reaction is of uncertain origin but it exists, upsetting the confidence of the theoreticians in the Kremlin and of Mao himself. Curiously enough, Mao referred recently to a statement on the subject by Madame Chiang Kai-shek. "China is a fertile ground for Communism," she said, "precisely because Christianity has never penetrated the country. But this fact has its converse side and leads us to believe that Communism will not be able to master Europe and America because of the fact that on these two continents Christianity has flourished as bamboo flourishes in China."

"Living according to realities" . . . this is Mao Tse-tung's motto and its consequence is that he plans to turn Peking into an antithesis of Rome just as in the political realm he has been turning it into an antithesis of Washington. His confidence is based on the "frivolity" of Christians, who frequently combat Communism without knowing fully its meaning, which amounts to firing a gun without a view-finder or looking into the distance through an unfocused telescope. The students of the Kun-Pa seminars are given systematic examples of this frivolity or Western near-sightedness. "The capitalists," their instructors tell them, "accuse us, without shading or modifying their statement in the least, of the fact that dialectical materialism absolute-ly denies the existence of something so evident as spiritual activity. They accuse us of believing only in matter and the senses. Such an accusation does not agree with reality. Dialectical materialism also believes in a sort of spirit, which it classifies as *the highest product*. Dialectical ma-terialism allows mental activity and the activity of the conscience. As a matter of fact, Lenin settled the question once and for all years ago when he stated that 'Matter and thought are equally real, and to call thought matter or to claim that matter embraces thought is to make a serious mistake.' "

No, Mao doesn't want to commit the same errors of underestimation that the West has committed, and he under-stands perfectly well that Christianity is his real enemy. Thus it is that in recent years, along with Russia, he has frequently employed an extremely shrewd stratagem which has caused numerous victims: namely, the claim that Com-munism and Christianity have many points in common and that really they are quite alike.

Nothing could be further from reality. Actually, the only resemblance between the two doctrines is this: in the Sermon on the Mount Christ spoke words which Communism later incorporated into its own Ten Commandments. The similarity ends there; in everything else the difference is fundamental. Christianity bases its strength on love, and Communism bases its on class hatred. Communism defends the thesis of evolution and applies it to the class struggle (remember that Marx drank deeply of Darwin's natural history), while Christianity integrates all of evolution in the creative act of God. For Communism, everything is "morally good" which helps to tear down the present economic system; for Christianity, everything is "morally good" which helps us to approach perfection, which in the final analysis consists in adoring the Father.

CUBA

1

CUBA, FULGENCIO BATISTA
AND THE U.S.A.

Cuba, island in the Antilles, situated to the south of the Tropic of Cancer, which, according to Baron Humboldt, has the shape of a crocodile, and which we have all thought of on occasion when putting sugar in our coffee, is the latest scene in the dramatic ballet begun in 1945 with the handing over of East Berlin to the Russian troops. Until now the Kremlin has proceeded to occupy mile after mile of our planet in Europe, Africa, and Asia. Cuba is its launching platform in America. Since Cuba, Khrushchev has repeatedly pointed to the chip on his shoulder, has done his shopping in Canada, and has threatened to overrun all Latin America. Mexico is nearby, just across the Strait of Yucatan. There are guerrillas in Colombia, in Venezuela, and in Bolivia. "Ché Guevara, with his musketeer's air, is from Argentina. Cuba is a constant topic of conversation and Fidel Castro, with his olive-drab uniform, his beard, and his voice magnetizes the masses, especially the peasants.

This whole phenomenon is of prime importance in view of the fact that the entire population of Cuba—six and a half million—is less than that of New York City, and it bears out an already accepted truth: that our generation lives under the sign of the all-powerful atom. Cuba, an atom-sized scrap of land floating between the Atlantic and the Caribbean, ironically contains enough concentrated energy to make an entire continent tremble.

There is a sentence of Giovanni Papini's which we might well apply to Cuba: "That which frightens the tiger, the moth falls in love with." According to Papini, this something is *fire*. Cuba is now fire; a number of moth-men, who would like to test their wings, are infatuated with it while, on the other hand, the tiger-men, who consider themselves strong, run away. Matches are scarce in today's Cuba, but the island is nonetheless pure fire because its "26th of July Movement" is fiery, just as its symbols are. Some revolutionary magazines have depicted Fidel with flames issuing from his mouth, like the Prophets, and even with a tongue of fire over his head! On the island there is a city called Cienfuegos ("a hundred fires"), and this was also the name of one of Fidel's intimates, Camilo Cienfuegos, who was a guerilla leader and militant anti-Communist and, as a result, "mysteriously disappeared over the ocean in an airplane accident," according to an official dispatch.

I disembarked in Havana at the beginning of July, 1961. The adventure attracted me strongly. My written observations on this subject have as their point of reference a thesis that is hard to dispute: namely, that the situation in Cuba, wild and Neronian, is the logical consequence of a chain of errors and horrors committed by the governments which preceded Castro.

Cuba is an island rich in its own right; Columbus described it emphatically as ". . . the loveliest land that human eyes ever beheld." Its annual gross income was large, not surprising in view of its great attractions for the tourist— "the industry without chimneys," as they call it in Mexico— and its temperament was political. It lies thousands of leagues from the Kremlin and venerated a maxim of the great Cuban liberator, José Martí, which says: "Changing masters doesn't mean being free." It seems unlikely that Cuba would have agreed to be turned into an armed camp if the temptation to do so had not been strong. The Cuban, guajiro or negro, is by no means in love with the rifle. If, thanks to Fidel, the distance separating Cuba from Moscow has disappeared, this is certainly due in part to the great psychological upheaval which is transforming the world, but more concretely it is due to the unsatisfactory previous administration, to the economic oppression exercised by the United States, and to statesmen like Fulgencio Batista, former Army stenographer.

Cuba, from the time it gained its independence at the turn of the century, has, except for slight exceptions, been a den of corruption. In 1958, on various city streets—the Prado, la calle de Virtudes, for example—it was common for the stranger to be offered fourteen and sixteen-year-old girls. Two hundred and seventy bordellos were operating in Havana, and more than seven hundred bars with "hostesses"; the gambling, lottery, and narcotics industries kept thousands of hands busy. Porters, taxi drivers and shoeshine boys were eager links between vice and the dollar. Meanwhile, family unity was gradually being undermined, factory workers plodded along without any professional stimulus, and a great part of the rural labor force had to look forward to four months of "dead time" once the harvest and the sugar-making were over, as happens too in Andalusia.

Nobody seems ever to have had an accurate, complete, and progressive concept of the nation's economic possibilities. The genius has been lacking, or perhaps simply the accountant, who might have brought the resources of the soil, the sub-soil and the sea into line with the vital pace of modern times and the needs of Cuba's people. And so it was that basic production of cereals declined, the fishing industry was neglected, mining was put at the mercy of the whims of American industry, and the raising of sugar-cane rashly came to account for 82 per cent of the total exports of the country. The national per capita income, while far superior to that of some other countries of Latin America, Africa, and Asia, was nevertheless low and stationary. The ratio of illiteracy climbed as high as 40 per cent in rural areas. In almost all the native huts lighting was provided by oil lamps, and there were no installations for water or of sanitary facilities. But above all the country lacked coherence, effective use of energy, and that joy which citizens feel when they know themselves to be co-workers in a common enterprise.

When someone says today: "How well people lived in Cuba before," he is actually telling a sugar-coated half-truth, just as the frequently overheard statement: "How gay Havana was in those days!" is not the whole truth. A third of the nation lived well, and Havana indeed had a certain superficial gaiety, but the country by no means enjoyed the sort of well-being that an honest and competent administration could have provided. The INRA (National Institute of Agrarian Reform) and Ché Guevara now claim, with statistics in hand, that the Cubans went hungry. This is likewise an inaccuracy; rice and beans were never lacking on any table. But the truth is that the bulk of the economy was controlled by shady corporations like Zapata's and produced a disturbing number of multi-millionaires and restricted beaches. The same thing was true of the Treasury Bureau as of the country's fauna: it was poor in quadrupeds and rich in birds and insects. Some of these birds were birds of prey and behaved like the parasitical coconut-crab, which climbs the coconut tree and eats its fruit.

Is the sequel so surprising? Lenin's best ally was the Czar; Communism has advanced because capitalism is as cold as a chunk of marble and has shown itself to be incapable of solving the problem of malnutrition and ignorance. Nor has it achieved, in spite of its practically unlimited resources, that spiritual development which the apathetic and fatalistic people of the world are entitled to under the law of brotherhood. Capitalism has not conceived of man as an end but rather as a means or instrument. Just as from high up over the clouds in an airplane one sees only silhouettes, so too from the vantage point of a Board of Directors one frequently sees only adding machines. England has dominated half the world without ever really coming to terms with it. Belgium has given up its mission in the Congo without having done away with cannibalism. Practically the only things that the civilized countries have sent into the desert and tribal areas have been teams of engineers and jeeps full of police. Every once in a while the figure of some missionary or doctor stands forth like a great dignified elm, rising above its surroundings. But Farouk, the Aga Khan and the "petroleum kings," all of them fond of dates, have been the crack through which discontent has leaked and assumed the proportions of a tidal wave. Pouring in on the crest of this discontent have been Marx, Engels, Lenin, Stalin and Khrushchev. Actually, without noticing it, the big monopolies have been manufacturing arms even if they were manufacturing medicines, until the day that the right leader appeared, with or without beard, trained in Moscow and ready to turn these arms over to the people, urging them to "do justice."

This appears to be the only way to explain how a creed as unnatural as dialectic materialism could have run up its flag in so many places. The great, almost legendary skill of Communism lies in the fact that it penetrates man in spite of going against his most deeply rooted instincts. It has no trouble attracting followers, despite its denial of all that is most intimate and essential to man: the right to choose his own course, personal initiative, the right to private property, freedom of thought, expression and association, and the practice of religion. The Communists have noted the paradox originally applied to Christianity—Chesterton wrote that one of the proofs of the divinity of Christ stems from the fact that He managed to popularize a doctrine which controlled the impulses: "He sold soap which doesn't wash" —and they frequently insist that Christ was the first Communist.

In the case of Cuba, the Americans have been the rude and greedy colonizers, and Fulgencio Batista was Fidel's best ally. The Yankees began to mortgage Cuban sovereignty as soon as Cuba freed herself from Spain, as soon as the last of the Spanish troops left the island. This took place on January 1, 1899. In clause 4 of the pact between Cuba and the United States it was agreed that once peace was restored the United States would renounce all control or jurisdiction over the island and would hand over to the natives "the fullness of powers." Nevertheless, shortly afterwards the so-called Platt Amendment was added to the Constitution; it provided for the rental of Guantanamo Bay to the United

States for the establishment of a naval base; the right to intervene "for the maintenance of an *adequate* government for the protection of life, property and individual liberties" was also guaranteed. In the economic field, American interference began with the purchase of land. The United Fruit Company alone bought 175,000 acres. Gigantic mills were built, railroads started, etc. The labor problem was solved by importing thousands of Haitians, Jamaicans, and Chinese coolies, who were housed in big barracks.

For sixty years, that is to say, throughout this century, the United States has done in Cuba and for Cuba what the Cubans themselves would never have done, but in return has received excessive profits and has not particularly bothered about the complexions of the people, or the curvature of their spines, or about their coffins. Cooperative Cuban politicians have not been lacking; all over Cuba, their statues have now been pulled down or melted "to make children's toys," and their names are pronounced with the same hatred as the names of the Cuba American Sugar Company, the Cuban Sugar Company, and General Sugar, and with the same vehemence used to describe Wall Street bankers.

The purpose of this essay is not a tedious recounting of facts and figures of production and buying power but it should be pointed out that in 1958 Cuba was economically dependent upon the United States without just compensation; the same situation is true and consequently equally dangerous in almost all of Latin America. The treaties making this situation in Cuba possible were objectively reasonable and the salaries paid by the American companies were high, but such a state of affairs nipped in the bud any genuine national emancipation and clearly gave little hope for the future, since it made no progress toward solving the vital educational and anthropological problems of the island.

Naturally, Fidel Castro has not solved the problem; he has simply turned Cuba over to another master, who lives far away in the Urals. Where the "imperialist Yankees" once relaxed and enjoyed themselves one now finds Russian, Czech, and Yugoslav diplomats and technicians, and even Chinese, surprisingly similar to the coolies imported years ago. The ships docking at Havana no longer bring refrigerators, television sets, and tourists but instead bring arms and petroleum, in exchange for sugar, tobacco, and coffee. Salaries have declined, the Revolution demands overtime and even obligatory participation on Sundays and holidays, in sugar harvesting or military training and parades. There is little soap and air conditioning is beginning to be scarce, but there is no scarcity of promises! "We shall win," "We are fighting for a better future." "Let our children not have to suffer what we suffered." The land has not been divided among all the peasants; in fact, the Cuban agrarian reform has passed directly into a totalitarian collectivism, without individual sharing of the profits. But this makes no difference, because the common good, according to the words of Dr. Castro, is based upon administration by the state, and the state is the people, whereas the big landholders were all either Cubans protected by Batista or else Yankees.

In short, Fidel Castro, who has based his revolution on agrarian reform, is following in the footsteps of the infamous Mafia, the organization founded in Sicily a hundred years ago which also employs the death sentence and whose reason for coming into being was the defense of the peasants against the landowners.

As for Fulgencio Batista, it is practically impossible to find anyone to defend him, even among the ranks of the anti-Castro factions. In the political sphere he did not confer on the nation a single institution with prospects of solidarity. In his hands everything, including the Army, became corrupt. On the social plane he never once aimed at basic goals, for which reason he became known in certain towns in Camagüey as "El Indiferente." On the economic level he consented to misapplications of funds of horrifying proportions. Batista, who also had a mansion in Daytona Beach, lived surrounded by a cohort of unscrupulous public officials—in Cuba they were called "botelleros" ("bottlers") and in Mexico, "aviadores" ("flyers")—whose siphoning of the federal coffers was implacable. In addition, the dictator, who needed many bodyguards, was a nepotist and protected the easy money. The Cuban people were shocked when, in 1960, Fidel Castro displayed in the Pasos Perdidos Hall of the Capitol "part of the personal treasure which Batista and his underlings had to leave behind when they fled abroad." According to Castro there was "a gold fan which weighed forty pounds, belonging to Batista's eldest son, Papo. There were silver trays over four feet long, and a six-thousand piece set of china. There was a gold-plated bed and a lamp of baccarat crystal." And in a position of prominence was displayed "the solid silver urinal used by Batista."

However, where Batista reached his zenith—*Fulgencio* means "resplendent"—was in matters of repression. As soon as Fidel set foot in the Sierra Maestra and it was seen that the peasants believed in him and were helping him, Batista began organizing expeditions and dragnets whose cruelty can be proved beyond a doubt. Especially in regard to the activities of his police, his trusted officers known for being "trigger-happy," it is difficult to find words to describe their ruthlessness. Some of them undoubtedly enjoyed their work, since the corpses to be "made an example" were left unburied on the sidewalks, the whip and the shackle were used regularly, and castration was re-established, as in Nazi Germany. But these were the dictatorship's last desperate moves. Every victim earned Batista ten enemies. Not only did he lose all popular support but even among the bourgeoisie and the administrative minority, volunteer-saboteurs were recruited; many of the present "counter-revolutionaries," both those inside Cuba and those in Miami, exhibit scars from the days when they fought against Batista. The Church denounced the situation; the Army, forced to defend a dying cause and to fire against the peasants, who were joining the rebels in growing numbers, preferred to surrender at the close of 1958 to the columns of guerillas advancing from the eastern provinces.

Cuba is one of the most curious and inexplicable dramas of our time. Fidel's Argentine comrade, Ché Guevera, could write a tango entitled: "Cuba, the Nation Forever Betrayed." Castro appeared in Escambray to be the "definitive solution" and the beacon which would illuminate the life of the island. He was at once a politician, an intellectual —he wore thick glasses, which he took off the day he achieved victory—and an economist. And in addition he was a fighter. His program was a model of simplicity: restore the democratic Constitution of 1940. His intentions were a model of purity: once the country was back to normal and peace was restored, he would call free elections. His words sounded like a Mozart melody: he would turn the army barracks into schools—"Arms? What for?"—and he would sell out the country to neither the Yankees nor the Communists. He would respect Cuba's traditions.

The deception has been unprecedented. The day that Fidel entered Havana, under the protection of Our Lady of Charity of Cobre, a group of armed men, bearded and dressed in olive drab, with rosaries hanging around their necks, held up a big banner which read: "Unconditionally with Fidel!" It was on this word, "unconditionally," that Fidel's recognition as leader of the nation rested. The endless speeches he had made in the Sierra against Trujillo of the Dominican Republic, against Duvalier of Haiti, against Somoza of Nicaragua, against Stroessner of Paraguay, etc. were all buried under the phrase "Unconditionally with Fidel." At that moment the latest and most tyrannical betrayal in Cuba's history began. The beacon changed color. Not only was the Constitution of 1940 not re-established, not only were free elections never called—Fidel would later observe: "Elections? What for? We would win an absolute majority"—but to top things off the schools were turned into army baracks. All of Cuba's traditions—philosophy, religion, the University, forms of life and even of diet would one by one be replaced by others without the slightest link to the Cuban people, and the government would sell out to Moscow for a song.

"That which frightens the tiger, the moth falls in love with." Fidel, a bearded moth who flies in a helicopter, has fallen in love with himself and with the Communist Party, his protector. But the tiger—the Cuban nation, Cuban history—fears him. The Cuban tiger is frightened. It lives huddled up on the island which is shaped like a crocodile, to the south of the Tropic of Cancer. Three hundred thousand bayonets and a Defense Committee in each building keep guard on it and intimidate it. When José Martí wrote: "Changing masters doesn't mean being free," perhaps he was thinking of Fidel. And maybe the same was true of

Ortega y Gasset when he wrote in *The Revolt of the Masses* that ". . . where mass man has sprung up, the sort of man turned out in a hurry and based on nothing more than a few abstractions," life has taken on "the sad aspect of a strangling monotony." "This mass man is a man previously emptied of his own history, without any sense of the past and thus obedient to all the so-called 'international' disciplines; for this reason he is always ready to pretend to be anything at all. He has only appetites, he thinks that he has only rights and no obligations; he is the man without *noblesse oblige—sine nobilate*—a snob."

2

PORTRAIT OF FIDEL

Fidel Castro Ruz was born in Mayarí, Oriente Province, on August 13, 1926, the same year that Ruiz de Alda, Durán and Ramón Franco crossed the Atlantic for the first time in a hydroplane from southern Spain to Argentina, and the same year that the Scotsman Baird invented television.

Castro, who today owns a country home outside Havana very near the former Hemingway home, is a living contradiction and has been showered with epithets from all quarters. To the exiles in Miami he is the Hyena, the Traitor, the Infidel. To his thousands of fanatics he is the twentieth century Simón Bolivar, the Liberator, or simply Fidel. Nikita Khrushchev calls him "my friend." The Spanish nuns expelled from Cuba identify him with Lucifer. Captain Bayo, famous in the Spanish Civil War, still calls him "my pupil," recalling that in 1955, in the Chalco mountains of Mexico, he taught him guerilla warfare. Ché Guevara, a medical doctor by profession, frequently calls him "Doctor Castro." He would be mistaken for a cyclone if the meteorologists didn't always give women's names to cyclones. His political and demagogical history, were it to end today, would resemble an explosive mixture of Buffalo Bill and Hitler, or Buffalo Bill and Nasser.

Physically, he is a slightly spongy giant, with a noble head and vigorous features—although his profile loses authority through the curve of his forehead and nose resembling that of a ram—and lastly, he has an intelligent and sarcastic smile. Sometimes he has only to slap on his fatigue cap or start to gesture to become suddenly and unexpectedly vulgar. When he concentrates, his gaze becomes a bit misty. When he gives orders, his eyebrows obstinately knit together. When he lights a cigar, one would say that he is mad with ambition. Describing Fidel is as hard as forgetting him. Chaotic and delirious, he can suddenly take on a certain majesty.

Fidel was born on a sugar plantation belonging to his father, Angel Castro, a Spanish immigrant from Galicia who made a fortune in sugar and timber. When Fidel was born, this fortune was estimated at about half a million dollars. Fidel is the son of Angel Castro's second wife, Lina Ruz Gonzáles, and he has four brothers, among them Raúl. His native district, Mayarí was overrun with squalid huts. "Around my house there was nothing but injustice," Fidel has declared; "the earth burned and these huts determined the course of my life."

Fidel's father was Catholic and so the boy was sent to the parish school and later to a boarding school in Santiago. He completed his preparatory schooling in Havana, at the Jesuit Colegio de Belén. Some of his schoolmates have described the Fidel of those years as a turbulent youth, an excellent actor and very fond of playing with firearms, for which he was punished regularly. His favorite sports were basketball and baseball. He avidly read the works of Martí, the liberator of Cuba, and anything having to do with American history. His vitality was overwhelming and he had a gift for words; he also had some sort of need, undoubtedly very deep-seated, to break with the order established by others and by custom. Nevertheless, nobody could have imagined that the day would come when he would be putting machine-guns in the hands of Cuban youths and persecuting the Catholic Church. He liked to move objects from one place to another. He liked to change friends. He was not very punctual.

This description seems to be borne out by the mention inserted in the class-book of the Colegio de Belén the year Fidel graduated, 1945: "He always distinguished himself in any courses connected with arts and letters. He was a real athlete, ever defending the school colors with courage and pride. He has known how to win the admiration and affection of all. He will study law and we do not doubt that he will fill the pages of his life with brilliant passages. Fidel has good qualities and will surely be a man of action."

Fidel Castro began to show himself to be a born agitator when, after finishing his high-school program, he entered the University to study to be a lawyer. In every meeting he spoke out passionately and he could be expected to be present at any protest demonstration. He was obsessed by the figure of Trujillo, the Dominican Republic's dictator, whom he called "a reincarnation of feudal despotism." In 1947, true to his convictions, he joined a secret expeditionary force of three thousand men whose object was to invade the Dominican Republic and overthrow Trujillo. This was Fidel's first guerilla action and it turned out to be a sad failure; Cuban naval vessels intercepted the operation and the young law student, just turned twenty-one, was forced to jump overboard with two companions and swim three miles to shore through shark infested water, to avoid being captured.

Back in the University after this escapade, he plunged into political life, helping to organize a committee to combat racial discrimination at the University itself, where negro students were excluded from the athletic teams. Castro was governed in this enterprise, as in so many others, by one of José Martí's sayings: "A man is more than white, more than mulatto, more than negro. Being Cuban is more than being white or mulatto or negro." At the same time, what was to become his "revolutionary constant" was already developing within him: anti-Yankeeism. The United States' "economic imperialism" kept him awake nights. His second guerilla action—a personal part in the so-called "Bogota coup" in 1948—is sketchy and confusing in every detail except for the fact that he passed out anti-American leaflets in the Colón Theatre. Fidel was thrown out of the theatre by the police and later, in the Claridge Hotel, a considerable quantity of propaganda material belonging to him was confiscated.

In 1948, before completing his studies, he married Mirta Díaz Balart, a Liberal Arts student at the University; eleven months later she gave him a baby boy, who is currently in Moscow. Mirta Díaz's father was a conservative and an influential man, and supposed that his son-in-law's political scarlet fever was merely a passing fancy. But Fidel stuck to his course and soon became president of the Federation of University Students.

He graduated from the University in 1950 and opened his law office in Havana. In accord with Lenin's prophetic words that "only intellectual or professional revolutionaries will be able to redeem the working class," his clientele was composed mainly of workers, peasants, and political prisoners. He wrote doctrinaire articles for the newspaper *Alerta* in which he delighted in a political eclecticism that seemed genuine.

The year 1952 was decisive for Fidel Castro. He determined to run as a candidate for Congress in the elections announced for that year. But the election was never held because of a military coup which returned the former Army sergeant, ex-stenographer Fulgencio Batista to power. Fidel, using his juridical position as a platform, demanded Batista's imprisonment, accusing him of being a usurper; however, the courts rejected his demands again and again. Then, in line with Nietzche's statement that "the most dangerous transformers of society are those who want to transform it for the benefit of their children and grandchildren," he decided that the only means of molding the country to suit his taste was by revolution.

This was Castro's key moment. Rich, an attorney, married and with a child, he could have given up his plans for revolution and become a peaceful, law-abiding citizen, but his untamed personality was not to be suppressed. He found a passionate ally in his brother Raúl, who was already flirting with Communism. Raúl, shorter than Fidel and lacking his physical constitution, looked like his lackey and was known as "Raulito,' "Little Raúl." He walked around with volumes by Marx under his arm, was also anti-American and also spoke in furious terms of the misery of the wretched huts of his native Mayarí.

Their pact sealed, the brothers Castro devoted themselves for the next several years to the job of recruiting volunteers "to overthrow the usurper." They managed to round up two hundred men, a great many of them former students, and two women. This tiny "Rebel Army" began to train in the use of firearms and drew up a daring plan of attack. The scheme was to attack the garrison of Moncada on the outskirts of Santiago, second largest garrison in the country, at dawn on July 26; this is where the Cuban Revolution gets its name of the "26th of July Movement." The garrison was to be stormed, the two thousand soldiers inside overwhelmed and, once the insurgents were in possession of the machine guns, tanks and other armaments, a public call was to be made to the people of Cuba in the name of democratic principles.

The operation ended in a failure like the attempt to invade Santo Domingo. There was indeed a fight and blood flowed, but the "Rebel Army" was dispersed by Batista's patrols, who pursued the fugitives mercilessly. Their objective was to capture Fidel. Batista shouted it to the four winds, suppressed civil liberties and declared that for each of his soldiers killed in the attack, ten prisoners would be executed.

It was now the dictator's critical move. Instead of hushing up the skirmish at Moncada, he only succeeded in turning the rebels into heroes. So, when Fidel was captured, exhausted, in a hut in the Sierra near Gran Piedra, the whole country was disturbed. Fidel was sent to Boniato Prison and immediately became the object of an avalanche of petitions for clemency from all over, among which the foremost were those of his wife and family, and of the Archbishop of Santiago, who became his protector.

Batista, cornered, agreed to try Castro legally. The trial was set for the Emergency Court. Fidel, with his acute revolutionary instinct, sensed that this was the ideal chance to put his case before the people and really intensify the legend of the 26th of July. With his hands chained together, he was driven in a special police jeep to court the first day of his trial, where he soon became insolent with the judges and turned the chamber into a platform for his own beliefs. His exceptional oratorical gifts and his legal background were the two props he skillfully used to keep public opinion aroused. Not only did he defend "the right to rebel against tyranny," citing appropriate texts of St. Thomas Aquinas, Luther, Milton, Rousseau, etc. but in addition he declared that Cuba "ought" to be happy and that the Cuban people's happiness was "the only price which could be paid for the blood of [his] dead companions." Little by little he began to turn the tables, to the point where he ceased to be a defendant and became instead a prosecutor. He accused the Batista regime of being illegitimate and termed Batista himself a "criminal and thief." In one of the sessions his testimony lasted five hours, a fact which kindled the masses when it became known. He set forth in detail the program of social redemption and patriotic independence which had motivated the members of the 26th of July Movement, and wound up his defense with a sentence which has since figured in almost all the Revolution's slogans: "Condemn me; it doesn't matter. History will absolve me."

He was sentenced to fifteen years in prison; his brother Raúl, to thirteen. Both were sent to the Isle of Pines, the "Treasure Island" of Stevenson's novel.

Fidel listened to his sentence without the slightest display of emotion and, once in prison, went on weaving his legend. During the seven months he spent in solitary confinement he had plenty of time to "meditate on Cuba's problems," on the strange and unexpected weakness of Batista, who had pardoned his life, and on Hitler's observation that ". . . a strong man is even stronger when alone." As soon as he was permitted to mingle with the other prisoners he began to teach them philosophy and history, christening his makeshift classroom the "Abel Santamaría Academy" in honor of one of the martyrs of the attack on the Moncada garrison. He himself studied English and the speeches of Edouardo R. Chibás, and redoubled in his own mind his determination to achieve the dream of a Cuba free from the economic oppression of the United States, "a country theoretically anti-colonial but whose empire, thanks to the dollar, is the most powerful in the world."

On May 2, 1955, Castro was granted amnesty; once again his wife had interceded in his behalf, but no sooner had she done so than she divorced him.

The day he arrived in Havana after being released from prison, Fidel was given a hero's welcome by the students. The legend was complete. However, Batista had learned a lesson and Castro soon found it convenient to leave the country for Mexico, where his brother Raúl was waiting for him and was already in contact with the Mexican Communist Party.

Once more the two Castros, more mature now than in 1954, made plans to "liberate Cuba, this time for good." Their difficulties were greater than ever, since they were now in exile, but their minds were made up and they were counting on receiving the necessary help. First of all they would have to obtain men, money, and arms. The plan, called the "Mexico Project," would have to be carried out with no slipups and with a stubborn determination.

In the space of a few months Fidel managed to round up eighty men—fewer than in the Moncada raid—among them Ché Guevara, an Argentine Communist who had fought against Perón and later, in Guatemala, with Jacobo Arbenz. Guevara's incorporation into the little band was to be a decisive step and provided the impetus and cohesion the Castros needed. He was calmer than they, more serene, more cerebral and studious. He would act as their balance-wheel and, moreover, would find in the Cuban cause the means of at last employing to best advantage his tremendous hatred for the United States.

"Project Mexico" needed a professional instructor and found him, suitably enough, in the person of Captain Bayo, exiled veteran of the Spanish Civil War and responsible for the famous landing attempt in Majorca. Bayo was of Cuban origin, having been born in Camagüey, and at this time was living in Mexico, managing a furniture factory.

Bayo took the eighty men to the Chalco district, to the mountains, where he introduced them to the fine points of guerrilla warfare. Such clandestine activity, and in a friendly country, made the novice guerrillas subject to constant arrests. Fidel was the least faithful of the students in class attendance, since he was constantly moving about in search of money and aid. The greatest success of his fund-raising drive was his trip to the United States itself, where he visited the Cuban colonies in Tampa, Miami, Union City, Bridgeport, and New York. Wealthy Cubans and Batista's American enemies were very responsive to his call and gave him some fifty thousand dollars. Later on, the donors on this list would refer to their actions as "Operation Hari-Kari."

The guerrilla seminar in the Chalco mountains ended in 1956. In the final exams, Professor Bayo awarded first prize to his star pupil, Ché Guevara. Fidel, who had steadily received nothing but good news from the island—an active fifth column was shouting "Viva Fidel" everywhere and awaiting his orders—felt himself master of the situation and decided to go into action, setting in motion the long-promised "invasion of Cuba."

Bayo opposed the project, holding that a force of eighty-two men was quite insufficient for a landing of any success. But Fidel remained firm. As soon as his contacts confirmed that everything was set in Havana, he gave the go-ahead; the plan was to synchronize the landing with a general strike and initiate a chain of sabotage actions. The whole adventure seems more like a children's tale than an authentic incident in contemporary history.

With this band of eighty-two aboard, the yacht "Granma" sailed out of the Tuxpán River bound for Niquero, west of Santiago de Cuba. However, luck deserted the little expeditionary force. The crossing turned into a horrible nightmare as a result of the excessive weight on board and the roughness of the sea. Finally, the vessel reached the Cuban coast, at an unknown and swampy point, in total darkness. In order to save themselves, the "invaders" had to abandon all their heavy equipment and reserve ammunition. "We shall head for the Sierra," Fidel declared; "we have reached Cuba and we shall triumph."

The party was discovered by Batista's army and chased over hill and valley and through sugar-cane plantations which were set on fire. Only twenty-two members of the expeditionary force were left alive, and ten of these were captured and sent to the Isle of Pines prison. A grand total of twelve persons reached Turquino Peak, high atop the Sierra Maestra; among them were Fidel, Raúl and Ché Guevara, who had received a bullet wound in his neck.

Once they reached the peak, Fidel announced, to the utter bewilderment of his companions: "The dictatorship's days are numbered!" It should be kept in mind that this same dictatorship had mobilized an armed force with a total strength of some thirty thousand men. Fidel also vowed that he would not shave, that he would let his beard grow until the day victory was achieved.

Castro's campaign, his move against Batista, lasted exactly two years, from Christmas of 1956 until New Year's Day of 1959, when Batista surrendered and fled the country. During these two years the information given out by the news agencies regarding the uneven fight taking place in Cuba was altogether contradictory. One minute they were declaring that the "intellectual rebel's" struggle was a lost cause and the next minute they released the information that his position was strengthened in the mountains and that his forces were growing in number.

This latter version was much closer to the truth. The peasants were indeed helping Fidel, forming concentric circles which reached farther and farther. Soon Fidel was able to boast of a field hospital and a newspaper called *Cuba Libre*. Some people compared him with the bandit Giuliano, but they were dealing with a very special Giuliano, who once again began quoting St. Thomas Aquinas and Milton, who established small schools and dispensaries in the areas he controlled, who improvised bakeries, butcher shops, a shoe factory, an arms plant, etc. He was a Giuliano who spoke in the slums a language the people wanted to hear: a "simple and practical" language of stereotyped ideas, driven home incessantly. He told them: "The land will be yours," "the Yankees will no longer exploit you," "soon you shall live like human beings."

On February 24, 1958, Fidel added to his collection of weapons his favorite of all: a radio transmitter, "Radio Rebelde," which began broadcasting from "the free territory of Cuba in the Sierra Maestra," and which in a short time gained listeners all over the island. Not long afterwards, he acquired an airplane, a C-64 loaded with heavy arms flown in by a childhood friend, Pedro Miret, which landed on a strip in the Sierra.

Was Fidel a Communist at this stage of the game? Did his supporters, among whom the New York Times was prominent, have any basis for supposing that he was hiding a tiny hammer and sickle in his whiskers?

This is a thorny question. Nobody has really been able to answer it once and for all; we must depend on the facts, and the facts can be interpreted in different ways. On one hand, Fidel persistently espoused a program of eclectic politics and stated that Stalin, then already dead, "had caused tremendous damage to the world-wide leftist movement." At one point he said—and these are his own words—"I wish to clarify here that I am not a Communist, because I am sure that the first thing that will be said when this campaign is over is that we are Communists." "The great problem confronting the world today is the fact that it finds itself in a position where it is being forced to choose between capitalism, which starves people to death, and Communism, which solves their economic problems but which suppresses those liberties so dear to man."

Besides, the Cuban Communist Party, called the "Popular Socialist Party," which had barely seven thousand members, had never supported Castro. In fact, one of its leaders, Marinello, had been a Batista government minister. On various occasions the Party labeled Fidel "Catholic and bourgeois" or "an inexperienced adventurer" and worse yet, completely boycotted the general strike which he tried to engineer in April of 1958. For his own part Fidel, who had no desire to mortgage his leadership, turned down Communist support when, in view of the imminent victory of Castro's forces, the Party sent its own guerrillas to the Sierra to jump on the band wagon. Later, after his triumph, he had his men throw the Communists out of the buildings they had occupied and he defied the labor unions. Thus, there was no public proof of any relationship between Castro and Communism except for their mutual anti-Yankeeism and their hatred of Batista. So far as religious policy goes, a detail which ordinarily would give us a good clue, it must be pointed out that the Sierra Maestra fighters, dubbed the "olive drabs" because of the color of their uniforms, wore rosaries and scapulars around their necks; Fidel, speaking over Radio Rebelde, invoked the protection of Our Lady of Charity and announced that on the day he achieved final victory a Te Deum of thanks would be sung.

There was, of course, the other side of the coin: among Fidel's closest followers there were several militant Communists, led by his brother Raúl, Ché Guevara, and Bayo, who was back in Mexico waiting for orders. None of them was eclectic or considered man's freedom to be a particularly essential quality. All this, added to Fidel's anti-Americanism, might have led one to suspect that, once Batista had been defeated, Cuba would drift into the Kremlin's orbit. Nevertheless, those who thought this way, and they were in the minority, were dismissed as defeat-mongers or as speculators on the dictator's payroll.

Be it as it may, Fidel was right: the dictatorship's days were numbered. The nucleus in Sierra Maestra prospered and grew, aided monetarily and militarily by the United States! There came a time when there was scarcely any danger at all in the mountains; the Revolution suffered more casualties among its saboteurs on the plains and in the cities than in the Sierra. Guerrilla leaders with special characteristics all their own began to appear: among others, Camilo Cienfuegos, Frank Pais, Faure Chomont, Commander Hubert Matos, etc. Only once in a while did Fidel's speeches strike an anti-democratic note; just as Nasser spoke of pan-Arabism, so too Castro spoke of liberating "all of Latin America."

The final and decisive offensive began in December of 1958, shortly after the spectacular kidnapping of the stockbroker Fangio. Palma Soriano was taken, the soldiers in the Moncada garrison refused to offer any resistance and surrendered, Sancti Spiritus and the port of Caibarien were captured and Santa Clara was surrounded. Batista, in a belated maneuver, sent an armored train to Santa Clara, but instead of thrusting rifle-muzzles through the slits, the troops stuck out white flags. On December 30, Santa Clara and Trinidad were captured. On St. Sylvester's Eve, under pressure by the military leaders at Camp Colombia, Batista surrendered and fled Cuba. It was exactly sixty years to the day—January 1, 1899—since the last Spaniards had evacuated the island.

Havana turned into a madhouse. Fidel did not enter the city immediately; he knew how to handle the masses and he was going to make them wait. The one who did enter, at the head of the "barbudos," was Ché Guevara, ". . . with his left arm in a sling and with a grave and a worried air about him," but in spite of his gravity the dam could not be kept from breaking: the capital went wild. The mobs, after opening the gates of all the prisons, burned the offices of the paper *Tempo,* sacked the Shell service stations and the offices of Iberia Airlines, K.L.M., and Air France, and especially vented their rage on the gambling casinos. The newsreel accounts of that mass orgy do not contribute anything special to the history of revolutionary riots: violent faces, massacres, pillage. There were, however, several distinctive notes to the Cuban outburst: the systematic destruction of all the slot machines and Ché Guevara's coolness as he set up his headquarters in La Cabana fortress.

Fidel did not enter Havana until January 8. The capital was jammed with passionate crowds awaiting his arrival. Fidel made his triumphal entry ". . . at the head of a column of two thousand men, and in his honor the ships in the harbor fired twenty-one gun saluates and the bells of all the churches pealed wildly!" The Liberator, riding in a jeep, proceeded to the Capitol, where he was received by Judge Manuel Urrutia, elected President of the provisional government, with which the United States had already established diplomatic relations and into whose empty coffers they had begun pouring sizeable loans.

This perhaps was Fidel's critical moment; the guerrilla war was over and, actually, everything had been relatively easy: eight years of stubbornness, of persecution, of disregard for death and of strategy. What would he give the Cuban people now, the Cuban people who had ransacked the Shell stations and the airline offices, the fourteen-year-old girls that a corrupt Havana had offered to foreigners, students, and farm hands? Now Fidel had before him the future, without time limit, and he had to fill that future with meaning. He discovered that he had to face a reality much more dangerous and subtle than Batista: peace.

The first thing he did was to take off his intellectual-looking glasses. The second was to find out whether his personal power over the masses was really unique, above all when he picked up a microphone or appeared on television, invented the same year he was born. The main thing he did was to set the stage for the drama of the eternal problem of love and hate.

Undoubtedly, love was a hard course to follow. It consisted of enduring pain sweetly. It meant demanding nothing, continuing to suffer inwardly. It meant studying the map of Cuba and thinking: "I must teach these six million people to reconstruct our nation according to justice, but using love as a basic and everlasting staff." But this meant renouncing his natural desires, including his legend. And there to prevent this was his own pride, and Ché and Raúl with their glasses raised in toast, and the frenzied chorus of thousands of voices, spread out through the Malecón, the Prado, and Zayas Park, urging him on.

Fidel Castro Ruz, the Bolivar of the twentieth century, Doctor Castro, the explosive mixture of Buffalo Bill and Hitler or Nasser, had reached the age of the predestined: thirty-three years. In Havana the rumor was circulating that during his period in prison Batista had had him castrated, but his immense vitality was a constant refutation of this rumor.

Fidel chose the path of hate. From the moment he embraced President Urrutia, he began to teach his people to hate. Hating was easy enough. It was sufficient to repeat, day after day, the list of errors and horrors committed by Batista and to tell the people: "You are the ones who must pull the trigger." Hating was voluptuous. It was contagious, just like airplane crashes seem to occur in series. In addition, hating could turn into a "program," "spirit," a national drive.

Fidel gave in to this temptation using, perhaps without even realizing it, the three classic weapons of the Kremlin: repression, spectacle, and the systematic use of lies.

The "Olive-green Revolution" now called up the firing squad. "In reality, the nation itself did the shooting." All over the island and right alongside the ramparts of La Cabaña fortress, the bullets began again to sing the same song they had sung under Batista, except that this time they were directed at other heads. Ché Guevara and Raúl Castro quickly took advantage of the situation by eliminating all the enemies of the Communist Party and replacing them with trusted subordinates; Raúl gave an accurate preview of his subsequent open sadism by giving personal orders for the execution of seventy-one military men in Santiago. At the same time a "purification" program was begun, which affected everything from pharmacies and hotels to the labor unions and the University, where a great many professors were dismissed. The G-2 Corps was organized, "Defense" Committees set up, and people were urged to inform on members of their families who had not "integrated themselves with the Revolution." The lexicon of the "26th of July Movement," which had had a certain poetic flavor in the Sierra, began to sound sterner: "Former government underlings, to the firing squad"; "The Revolution is strong medicine"; "Cardinal Arteaga is the chief instrument of Cuba's enemies." With a view toward the nation's children and grandchildren, the Rebel Pioneers and Rebel Youth groups were established. The Pioneers were children from seven to thirteen years of age, who were given an initiation in military training. The Young Rebels were youngsters from thirteen to seventeen, who were given firearms training and the chance to graduate.

As for spectacle, Fidel showed himself to be an accomplished master, perfectly adapted to the idiosyncrasies of his people. Once he was installed in his feudal manor, the "Havana Libre" Hotel (the ex-Hilton), where he acted over the heads of the government and signed decrees at will, he undertook sporadic visits around the island in jeep, helicopter, or even on donkey through the villages. Under his direction, the "Olive-green Revolution" mounted a propaganda campaign even more amazing than that accomplished in the Dominican Republic under Trujillo. The telephone operators answered with "Homeland or death," the radios blared "We shall win," and in all the offices appeared signs that said: "Be brief; we are 50 years behind the times." Millions of posters and pictures of Fidel blossomed on walls and in windows, and the militiamen wore emblems on their sweaters, their caps, the toes of their boots, and pasted slogans on tractors and even on ice cream cones! However, it was Fidel who reached the peak of spectacularity when he gathered together a million Cubans in Plaza Cívica in Havana for the so-called "Operation Truth." The object was to turn the multitude into a jury: a lesson in "direct democracy." "All those in favor of executing these petty functionaries, raise your hands!" A million hands filled the air of the Plaza. Later on, inspired perhaps by the Nuremberg trials, Fidel held his trials in the Sports Palace, with a capacity of eighteen thousand, where the testimony of children was readily admitted: "This man, this man, he killed my father!'

And finally, the third weapon, the systematic use of lies, "lies built around a tiny grain of truth," was quickly carried to paroxysms. The new state lied when it solemnly declared that projects frankly worthy of Jules Verne were quite attainable, when it demanded new taxes, when it postponed elections. The INRA (National Institute of Agrarian Reform) lied when it started "distributing" land and giving "property titles" and "bonds." The INIT (National Institute of Tourist Industries) lied when it pretended that the hotels still required white-gloved clerks and elevator operators. The press, already gagged, lied when it spoke about the successful racial integration and told the country: "We are fighting so that every Cuban can express his opinion freely." Fidel, obliged by the enormity of the budget to take steps not foreseen in the Sierra, lied when he tried to justify the confiscation of the telephone and electric companies. At the time of his trip to the United States in April, he lied when he stated: "The nation to the north, our rich northern neighbor, has understood our feelings."

This last lie was possibly the most transcendental of all, for the next step was already clear. The nationalization of wealth, directed by Ché Guevara from his office in the National Bank, inevitably had to affect American capital invested in Cuba, which would in turn lead to the breaking off of relations between the "rich northern neighbor" and Castro. That was exactly what happened, except for shipments of food and pharmaceutical products. Then Fidel went on lying: "Our treaty with the United States," he declared, "was the treaty of a shark and a sardine."

The consequences of the withdrawal of the "shark," who had previously refused to refine Russian petroleum, were not long in coming. Amid Ché Guevara's smiles and greetings, the first Soviet economists arrived in Cuba and Castro continued lying: "Negotiating with Russia does not mean going over to Communism. Cuba will deal with any country that makes her a reasonable offer." Thousands of Cubans began the exodus, among them some of Fidel's intimate collaborators, which gave him the excuse for another lie: "They're nothing more than garbage, imperialists in disguise, enemies of the people. Just pronouncing their names alone is enough to make us vomit." The Church began to show signs of restlessness at the one-sided screening of the book stores, the calumnies against priests and nuns, the offensive searches conducted in convents and chapels, and the plan to nationalize all schools. And Fidel went on with his lies: "There are many of us who profess the Catholic faith and kneel before our Patroness, Our

Lady of Charity of Cobre. The Revolution only persecutes those priests who turn their pulpits into counter-revolutionary soapboxes or who hide arms in the sacristy." The selection of people proven loyal to the "cause" for responsible positions resulted in the appointment of a shoemaker to be director of the Firestone factory. Fidel observed: "Running a factory is something anyone can learn; not everyone is a born revolutionary, however."

Fidel's evolution, his subservience to the directives of the Kremlin, were amazing, to say the least. Obviously, the attitude of the United States was hardly a sufficient reason in itself for such an evolution. Fidel gave in voluntarily to Communist pressure, just as for their part the Communists accepted good-naturedly Fidel's continued enjoyment of a personal aureole. It was a sort of middle-of-the-road agreement, which received official backing during Mikoyan's visit to Cuba in February of 1960. From that date on, events moved quickly. They started with the sugar agreement signed by Cuba and the U.S.S.R. and have continued since.

Summing up, then, we find that by the middle of 1960 hardly a single revolutionary principle proclaimed by Fidel in the Sierra was still in force. It had taken him only eighteen months to bring his country to a most enigmatic crossroads, which confused Cubans and foreigners alike, friends and enemies. One minute his 26th of July Movement was being called a "dictatorship of the peasants and workers," despite the fact that not a peasant or a worker occupied any important post in the government, and the next minute it was being described as a "humanistic revolution," although the "human" factor, man as an individual, did not figure in the official plan. In addition, in spite of the obvious despotism being practiced, Fidel continued to refer to his new state as an example of "direct democracy." In any event, one fact stands out clearly and undeniably: Fidel had not succeeded in giving his six and one half million Cubans the happiness they wanted. He had so overloaded his Revolution that it got stuck in the mud, just like the yacht "Granma." Fidel, riding his stallion of hate, had lost the peace.

He had lost it to such an extent that a real, threatening discomfort was seizing control of the island. It was taking hold to a degree that, had it not been for the confused shouting and declarations of the exiles in Miami, followed by the "declaration of invasion" and its resounding failure, Fidel would have fallen within a year. Unamuno once said: "Man must aspire to be a mirror." Fidel, dazzled by the looking glass of Mao Tse-tung, was gradually undermining his own monument.

The abortive invasion attempt breathed new life into the 26th of July Movement and its leader. Nevertheless, even had such an ill-fated invasion never been attempted, in spite of Fidel's errors it would be foolish and a mistake to underestimate the capricious Cuban leader's personality. Fidel, who currently wears two wrist watches and still never arrives anywhere on time, is unquestionably one of the most singular figures of our age. The observation about him in the Colegio de Belén yearbook hit the nail on the head: "He has good qualities and will surely be a man of action." Born in Mayarí, he took over an entire country, starting from scratch and in opposition to an unscrupulous Goliath. Despite his betrayal of the nation, he still has the support of an important sector of that nation. The Kremlin has brought him under its thumb but still cannot dispense with his leadership. He probably lacks the sturdy doctrine capable of carrying him through the reverses of fortune found in any epic, the durable strength to come out on top of the cyclone. However, as a direct revolutionary, a "modifier of the order established by custom and by other people," he is comparable to Hitler and Lenin.

Where is Fidel headed? Nobody knows. His classmates said of him when he was already an adolescent that he liked to "change things around" and "change friends."

3

---◆---

FROM NEW YORK TO HAVANA

People never fail to be surprised by the fact that the only passenger ships making regular calls in Havana belong to a Spanish line. Tankers, cargo vessels, and other commercial ships of all sorts are constantly arriving, flying the flags of Greece, Poland, Lebanon, Russia, Italy, etc., but the only passenger ships belong to the Compañía Transatlántica Española, founded in 1850, whose head chaplain was Father Jacinto Verdaguer, author of the "Atlantis" that was the inspiration and basis of de Falla's composition.

The Spanish Transatlantic Company was founded by Antonio López, marqués de Comillas, who had gone to Cuba as a boy to make his fortune; one would almost say that the line feels so attached to the waters of the Antilles that it does not want to break off its ties even under the present difficult conditions. What professional gallantry! More than 110 years of crossing the Atlantic, carrying men and women, the mail, good news and bad, create a habit and a responsibility not easily broken. But such gallantry is not a recent innovation: it has a precedent in an incident that took place at the time of the Spanish-American War. The first ship to enter Havana after Spain had lost the island belonged to the Compañía Transatlántica. Its arrival touched off a riot on the dock, with some Cubans shouting: "Viva Cuba!" and some Spaniards shouting: "Viva España!"; someone saved the day by shouting simply: "Viva la Compañía!" Everyone in the Caribbean knew that the "Compañía" was the Compañía Transatlántica Española. Naturally, the present maintenance of service has permitted the evacuation from Cuba of the Spanish residents persecuted by Castro.

The ship that carried me from New York to Havana in 1961, the "Guadalupe," commanded by Captain Alfredo Cuervas-Mons of Santander, belonged to this line. On the day we were to sail I went aboard and discovered that the passenger list was composed mainly of Cubans leaving the United States, some 250 altogether. There were also a few Mexicans, among them a man of about forty with obviously Indian features, who came up the gangplank wearing a summer cap and carrying a wooden suitcase and a guitar.

The presence of these 250 Cubans interested me enormously because I was deeply interested in their problem. Aside from some active "Fidelistas," expelled by the FBI, the majority of them were returning to Cuba voluntarily, to "integrate themselves with the Revolution," which had just "defeated the Americans" in the Miami-organized invasion attempt of April 17. Most of them were very excited. Their language was loud and extravagant and their voices filled the staterooms and passageways of the "Guadalupe" with jargon. The gigantic steel cranes of the pier lifted their cars, their refrigerators, and their washing machines high into the air and deposited them on the deck with a certain solemnity. A few of these families, after years of hard work in New York, Chicago, or Philadelphia, had saved a more or less considerable sum of money, which they carried lovingly with them.

As soon as the immigration officers had left the ship and the crew of the "Guadalupe" had pulled up the gangplank and thrown off the lines, the Cubans lined the rails and shouted at the dock workers below: "Cuba, sí; Yankees, no!" The stevedores, most of them Negroes, made gestures of obvious displeasure; some crossed their arms. Apparently, on the previous trip departing Cubans opened up with their insults before the ship had pulled away, while their luggage was still in Customs. The dock workers, in reprisal, had refused to load their autos and trunks.

At last the ship reached the tip of Manhattan and passed the Statue of Liberty; we were leaving New York. On the bridge, the Captain invited me to give a last look through the haze at this modern Babylon; I felt overcome by a strange sense of ill-being as I stared at the horrible and yet wonderful blasphemies of cement and steel which its architects had aimed at the skies. My stay in the United States had lasted almost six weeks. It was an unforgettable experience but, viewed as a whole, somewhat sad, since it had only confirmed my fears with respect to the myopia and immaturity of the "Colossus of the West."

For reasons which I shall explain in detail someday, I went to the States convinced that the sense of values governing the country was not capable of the defense of our historical heritage and, therefore, of halting the advance of Communism. I failed to find the necessary vigor so vital if we are going to give meaning and cohesion to the slippery complexity of these times. I did not find it in the

White House, or in Mr. Stevenson, with whom I had an interview, or in the United Nations, or in the foreign aid program, or in the moon projects, or in the atomic laboratories, or in the universities, or in the annual per capita income, or in the average citizen's "good faith" or in his amazing capacity for pitching in and working in harmony with his neighbors to create new sources of wealth, or in the articles of the Constitution, or in Jefferson's powerful words: "I guide my ship with Hope in the prow and Fear at the stern." The tide of the twentieth century was innundating those who, in many areas, occupied its highest peaks. The world is a reality far more esoteric than any "Perfect Salesman's Handbook."

Once we were on the high seas, life aboard ship became more normal. In the bars, public rooms, and around the swimming pool the inevitable cliques took shape. The passengers grouped together because of family ties or out of friendship; I struck up a friendship with the Indian-featured Mexican who had climbed the gangplank with a guitar in his hand. He was cautious in his speech but well-educated and sentimental. Within the space of a few months, he had visited Havana three times; his information would therefore be firsthand. Quite apart from the matter of Fidel Castro, he had barely a mediocre opinion of Cuba. "It lacks raw material, if you know what I mean. Look around at these people and tell me what you think." I asked him if he agreed with a curious opinion expressed by Paco Cossío in his book *A Hundred Years of Life at Sea,* that in the overall picture of Latin America the Spanish influence had been much more penetrating in those countries where Spain had a viceroy, such as Mexico and Peru, than in other countries, like Cuba, where she had sent merely captain-generals or representatives of the Finance

Ministry. "I have never thought of it that way," my friend answered. "It's quite possible he is right."

I observed the Cubans closely. The pandemonium went on, without respite for anyone. The children treated the ship's furnishings as though they were personal enemies of Fidel. The men seemed calmer but the women, wearing tightly-fitted trousers and all sorts of hairnets, clips, and pincurls, raised a tremendous tumult, especially in the pool, where they never paid attention to the hours posted. They looked at those of us in first-class with an emphatic aggressiveness. One of them, seeing me come out of the chapel one day, asked me if I were Spanish and whether I made my home in Franco's Spain. As soon as I answered yes, she gritted her teeth together and muttered: "Imperialist." Another woman came into the bar one day and, seeing me playing chess with the Mexican, observed wisely: "All's well that ends well."

The Mexican confessed that he felt a profound pity for these emigrants. "They don't know what's waiting for them. They're returning full of illusions, imagining that Fidel is going to receive them with open arms. What a laugh! The first thing they'll do to them when they get to Havana is change their dollars for Cuban pesos, at par. Do you get it? The years of hard work, all their savings, lost in a minute. Then, the payoff. They'll strip them from head to foot, since the Revolution is afraid of spies slipping in, and of people hiding microfilm somewhere. And that's that! If they're lucky, they may get to keep their cars."

The Mexican was a pessimist. In reality, he felt sorry for all of Latin America because of its backwardness and laziness. He had travelled it all over, from one end to the other, several times and had come to the conclusion that the "rew material" was lacking not only in Cuba but in all

the Spanish-speaking nations of America. "They are suited
for neither democracy nor dictatorship. And it's not merely
a question of money; it's that no two of these countries
seem to want the same thing. In Uruguay and Chile the
people want to own something of their own, property or
a business, but once they have it, they aren't happy either.
On the other hand, it seems to me the desire to become a
property owner is rare in Cuba. I don't know whether you
are familiar with the Nelson Survey made in 1945. Nelson
concluded that, before becoming property owners, what
the Cubans wanted were roads, schools, irrigation, living
quarters, and machinery. But even if you gave them all
that, it would not be a solution. The women would keep
on screaming like tropical birds and the kids would still
destroy the ship's furniture."

The "Guadalupe" ploughed on through the Atlantic
under a kindly sun. The Cubans whiled away their time
playing bridge, quoits, canasta, and dominoes, but spent
most of the time glued to their transistors, or requesting
rumbas and cha-cha-chas of the band leader, or reading
the arsenal of magazines and papers from Fidel's Cuba
which they had brought along with them in their suitcases.
These publications, which I had a chance to examine closely
—the yellowish paper and the poor quality of the printing
reminded me of the Soviet publications I had bought in
Helsinki—seemed to excite the Cubans terrifically. "Imagine, look at this," they exclaimed; "just listen to this."
Cuba Nueva talked about nuns who killed children, about
cardinals given over to orgies, and every time it referred
to Spanish priests in Cuba, it called them "the Falangist
clergy." *Vanidades* spoke of Norka, "the leading model in
Havana, who served guard duty with her rifle, dressed as
a militiawoman." *Inra* and *Obra Revolucionaria* devoted

entire pages to "How tractors are made in Czechoslovakia," or "How the blind are treated in the Soviet Union," etc. *Bohemia* demanded the creation of a hundred thousand new Defense Committees: "Committees in every factory, workshop, and building."

One of the Cubans, who spent all day lounging around in his swimming trunks, insisted on reading aloud to the ship's waiters and to a curious passenger of German origin who walked around giving everyone pocket combs. This Cuban got especially carried away by Sartre's and Simone de Beauvoir's declarations in favor of Fidel, which were reported extensively in all the papers and magazines. "What do you think about that, eh?" He also recited poems by Neruda and Guillén referring to the Cuban Revolution, standing up on his chair, as well as one by Alberti from which he deduced that "the generals are sinking the world."

The first night out, the emigrants gave a dance. They drank quite a bit and at the end a mulatto girl appeared with a little doll representing Kennedy which she began to stick full of pins; this drew a great shout of delight from the merrymakers. The Mexican told me that the girl had probably learned her trick in the "hillbilly" regions of the United States, where people still make little figures of their enemies and then stick them with pins to try to cause them some misfortune in real life. The Mexican gave special importance to the place of superstition in South American countries. "In South America, certain plants and amulets have more power than politics and theology. Superstition also favorably influenced Fidel's success . . . no, don't take it as a joke. Fidel was very clever to let his hair and beard grow. In Cuba there are many superstitions based on the hair. A long head of hair and a beard bring luck and are patriarchal, an attribute of the chosen of God, a symbol of the prophets."

The emigrant's ball had an unpleasant ending. At a very late hour they had to be called to order; they had caused some damage in the second-class bar and threatened a waiter. Then it was that we discovered that they all had a leader, a young man with a triangular face, widely separated eyes and pointed chin, who was travelling in first-class, of all places, with his wife and a nine-year-old son. The Mexican, who was turning into a priceless guide, explained to me that this "leader" was one of many Cubans resident in the United States who had been charged by the Revolution with recruiting immigrants. "This fellow worked in a furniture factory in Chicago. He is in charge of the expedition, and is sure to nip this misbehavior in the bud."

He was right; the "leader" called his charges together for an "exchange of impressions" to be held the following day. Dying of curiosity, I asked for permission to attend, since the rules of the ship gave me a perfect right to do so.

I fell asleep at once that night and dreamt that Fidel's helicopter was flying overhead and landing on deck. At eleven on the dot the following morning I headed for the second-class salon, which had been chosen for the pep rally.

The place was full. The women had put on black Revolutionary berets and had hung effigies of Fidel on their bosoms. In the place of honor were hung banners and inscriptions reading: "Cuba, sí; Yankees, no." "Homeland or death." "We shall win." The atmosphere, as they waited for the arrival of their "leader," was one of fellowship and good spirits. There was a Negro wrestler getting big laughs out of the audience with his mimicry and deep voice.

When the leader appeared at last with his wife, son, and a sort of secretary with an obstinate expression, nobody stood up but they all applauded. Looking as though he meant business, he made a motion for silence and, without any beating around the bush, warned his listeners, in the name of the Revolution, to "behave aboard the ship in a manner worthy of revolutionaries." "I trust that from here to Havana there will be no repetition of last night's unpleasantness. If the Cuban Revolution enjoys prestige and stirs up admiration in the other countries of Latin America, this is because it is a revolution of fairness and honor. Fidel has given us an example, respecting even his enemies, even the 'worms,' mixing with them at the trials and in front of the television cameras. Besides, don't forget that the waiter you provoked last night is our friend, a worker like ourselves; what you did last night might get him into trouble with his employers. Of course, I have no business telling you what to do; I'm just another revolutionary like yourselves, without anything to recommend me except my love for Cuba. But since you have put your trust in me, I feel obliged to speak to you this way. I know you will understand and pardon me."

Having received their promise to obey, the leader went on to give some instructions. "We'll have to pass a medical examination before landing in Havana. It's bothersome but the Revolution insists on it because one of the goals Fidel has set is real hygiene, effective public health, to do away with the whole set of diseases like polio and typhus which exacted such a toll from the island during Batista's dictatorship." Then he informed them that he had been able to raise quite a bit of money in the United States for the Revolution among Cuban families and sympathizers and that he would hand it over to the Cuban authorities in Havana harbor. He next suggested that a collection be taken up right then and there, taking advantage of the fact that they were all together. Six young girls came forward with trays. One of them stopped in front of me and I remained motionless. She stared at me insistently and I finally shook my head. At this her Caribbean eyes dilated and, in a voice brimming over with genuine hatred, she muttered: "Imperialist!"

Shortly afterwards the leader announced how much had been collected; it came to $470. There was a great ovation and everyone stood up. It must be admitted that there was something terribly sincere in all this, an absolute giving of oneself to the "cause." The national anthem was sung, nobody gave a closed-fist salute, and the meeting ended with shouts of "Homeland or death!"

I went out on deck and, leaning over the railing, watched the endless motion of the sea, while the loudspeakers gave some male singer the change to proclaim his praises of the beauties of Naples. We were getting close to the Tropics. The light was silvery and a hot vapor rose from the water. The ship's paint, the tar, and the red lead gave off an intense odor.

Before long Sartre's admirer came up to me and said he was nervous. Shortly afterwards, the extravagant German-born American, who had apparently been a prisoner in Europe during the war, came by, gave me a comb, and disappeared. And then, the leader himself, with his triangular face and serious manner put in an appearance. He excused himself for bothering me, but someone had told him I wrote books, that I was a Spanish intellectual and, furthermore, he had just seen me in the Cuban get-together. He wanted to talk to me, to exchange impressions, because this was what the Cuban Revolution needed:

that all the world's intellectuals ~discover the truth, like Sartre. "There are so many lies being printed, at a dollar per word!"

"What is the truth?" I asked him.

"Get off in Havana and see for yourself," he replied.

"Get off in Havana? Not a chance!"

"And why not?"

"I don't like machine guns on every corner."

"Machine guns? We were invaded and we had to defend ourselves. That's logical, isn't it? But if you'd like to go ashore, I'll see to it that you are given guarantees."

"Thank you, but I prefer ports where I can go ashore without guarantees from anyone."

He did not change his expression in the least. "So, then, you are against Fidel. . ."

"I am anti-Communist."

He offered me a cigarette. "And what does that have to do with it? The Cuban Revolution is not Communist."

"No? On May 1 Fidel proclaimed the Socialist Republic of Cuba."

"Socialist!—you said it yourself," the leader shot back. "Socialism, not Communism. Communism doesn't exist yet; it doesn't exist anywhere, not even in Russia."

"I know, I know all the little word games by heart. 'Communism is the final stage, the perfect state, and to reach it we shall have to wait many years yet.' "

He leaned over with his elbows on the railings as though my lack of comprehension had made him feel sorry for me. "Fidel has never been a Communist."

"But he certainly acts as though he were, and Guevara and Raúl are Communists."

"Yes, of course, those two are. And Carlos Rafael is, too."

"Who is Carlos Rafael?"

"You don't know of him? My goodness! He is an Economics professor and editor of the newspaper *Hoy* in Havana. Carlos Rafael . . . how can I put it?" The leader smiled. "He has even grown a little goatee in order to look more like Lenin."

Now it was my turn to smile. All this confirmed the information I had been given in New York and Washington. The Marxist theorist and dialectical adviser of the Cuban Revolution, then, was Carlos Rafael Rodríguez, whom the exiles in Miami called "the little red billy goat." The intellectual classification of the Cuban rebels usually went like this: Carlos Rafael, Ché Guevara, Fidel, Raúl. Ché surpassed Fidel in elasticity; he was just as much at home running the National Bank as directing the Agrarian Reform. Fidel, on the other hand, surpassed Ché in demagogic magnetism and in a sense of timing. As for Raúl, Little Raulito, he was the capricious one of the lot. He didn't have hair, couldn't grow a beard, and so he tried to grow a pigtail. He had an effeminate, sadistic air about him. In the Sierra Maestra he had risked his own life to save Fidel's, but once in power he wouldn't hesitate, along with Ché Guevara, to tighten the screws if Fidel opposed their Communist take-over.

My conversation with the leader, a true prefabricated man, typical product of Soviet literature, spread over two hours, near the swimming pool, under a self-confident sky. His thesis was clear; we capitalists could do nothing to stop the march of Socialism and its final goal, the establishment of Communism all around the world. A billion and a half people—almost two-thirds of humanity—were undernourished, ill-housed, and practically illiterate. Capitalism attacked and smothered helpless countries with its two favorite weapons: monopolies and colonialism. Communism, which had opened the proletariat's eyes, offered the solution. It was a hard fight and, for the time being, one had to resort to promises, but the promises would be kept. In 1917, at the time of the triumph of Bolshevism, Russia was a miserable country with no future; by 1961, it was a world power and the home of astronaut Yuri Gagarin. The same thing would happen in Spanish-speaking America. The Yankees exploited the oil wells, as for example in Venezuela, and flooded the market with their own products, but the tide was beginning to turn. South America had stoned Nixon and would stone Kennedy the first chance it got. In Cuba, many hardships were in store for the people as a result of the United States boycott. Fidel said: "We have to tighten our belts," but by 1963 at the latest they would start to reap the benefits of Soviet aid and the first generation of the new Cuban youth would be ready. "My son is nine and is anxious to get to Havana in order to join the Rebel Pioneers," the leader assured me. "They're mistaken in Miami if they think they can make us surrender out of hunger and hardship. If we have to, we'll eat malanga roots. I don't like malanga but I'll eat it and I can say the same for my wife and son, and for all of us on this ship who are Cubans, and for 70 percent of the Cuban people.

"Humanity's future is not dependant on resignation or on a belief or faith in heaven, like the pie in the sky the priests try to sell us on. The future we are interested in is right here on earth and what we are counting on are the modern scientific discoveries. It is a disgrace that mankind is still suffering from hunger when all the inhabitants of the earth would fit into an area smaller than Cuba if they were all sitting down."

I interrupted, in a controlled tone of voice: "Russia isn't going to solve anyone's problems, much less yours. She will exploit you more than the Americans ever did. The Russians will carry off all your resources and your spiritual independence in exchange for oil and arms."

For the first time the leader became irritated. Holding up his cigarette, he stared at me intently, his triangular face even more pointed: "Now you're talking like the Nazis."

I went on: "In Western Germany I have seen hundreds of fugitives from the Eastern Zone. Their gloom is unbelievable. Everything to do with Russia is gloomy. Communism gives no importance to human life. It thinks nothing of transplanting entire populations, it urges people to inform on their brothers, it lies ceaselessly. There, the monopoly is the state, and the most colonialistic country on earth is Russia."

"It's easy to tell you listen to all of Franco's speeches," the Cuban remarked. "Nobody has ever bothered as much about human life as Socialism is doing now. The thing is that we must worry about everyone and not just a select few. Sadness in the East? In Cuba, no one has ever laughed so much as people do these days at the swimming pools and clubs. Fugitives from the East? I can only speak of Cuban fugitives. I knew quite a few in Chicago; they were undesirables. And why shouldn't we inform on our brother if he is anti-patriotic? As for lying, I don't know of a single government, a single political system that doesn't. Do you think they don't lie in the United States? Do you mean to tell me De Gaulle in France and Nehru in India don't lie? The people can know only part of the truth. I myself told my fellow Cubans that we had collected $470 when the truth is we didn't raise even $300. I told them that to pep them up. The trouble is you're drugged with materialistic ideas."

The leader continued talking. He was quite enthusiastic over an article published by the INRA about a successful experiment in Bologna, Italy, having to do with the fertilization of the female ovary outside the body, *in vitro.* "That's the right course. . ." I asked him whether, being Cuban, he felt anything toward Spain; shaking his head, he answered: "No, I'm sorry, not a thing." I asked him about religious persecution in Cuba—I had received reliable reports about violations in Camagüey and even brainwashing—but he denied that any such religious persecution existed. "In Havana, if you decide to go ashore, you'll see the churches open." I asked whether he himself had any religious beliefs and he answered, with a smile: "None whatsoever. Within a hundred years all those superstitions will have disappeared." Later on he spoke of Yuri Gagarin: "What do you think about that? He's gone around the world!" He went on to tell me that control of the United States is in the hands of the Jews and that the Jews are responsible for the big increase in abstract art, as well as for fatalistic and pornographic motion pictures. "The Jews are making use of anything which destroys the personality." Finally, he again prophesied the "Cubanization" of all Latin America and once more invited me to disembark in Havana, where I could "be an eyewitness to the miracle being performed by the Olive-green Revolution."

Our discussion broke up at meal time; my Mexican friend came over to my table in the dining room and whispered: "How was the chat? Nikita is a nice guy, right?" The ship's officers told me the Cubans had behaved properly all morning. The hairdresser and the barber had even received a lot of tips. That afternoon there would be a

"Maraca recital" by the Negro wrestler, and the women were going to sew more flags and effigies of Fidel in preparation for the arrival in Havana. To top things off, the mulatto girl who had stuck pins in the voodoo doll representing Kennedy, was going to perform sleight-of-hand tricks.

The ship enjoyed a few peaceful hours until suddenly we noticed a strip of land to starboard; it was Florida. Soon we would be opposite Miami, where so many Cuban exiles lived and where the famous invasion attempt was conceived. The water was filled with yachts and luxurious pleasure-craft. On shore, we could see an endless line of cars crawling along.

The thought of being so close to Miami made the Cubans aboard the ship lose their composure again. They shouted in the direction of the hotels and beaches and, at a safe distance, insulted the many fishing boats, calling them "imperialists." The leader's secretary, who wore a monumental beret, exclaimed: "Phew! That coast smells of worms!"

"Worms . . ."; this was the term that Fidel had applied to the volunteers who had "invaded" Cuba in April. The Mexican seemed to be up on all the details of the operation, since he told me aspects I hadn't known. I knew, like everyone else, that the success of the invasion plan—approved first by the Eisenhower administration and later by the Kennedy administration—was taken for granted, as it consisted of simultaneous landings at different places on the island, backed up by air support and the massive action of a fifth column. I also knew that the attempt had failed because, at the last minute, in spite of repeated statements by the President that "We shall not abandon Cuba," and that "We shall not allow a Communist installation ninety miles from our shores," the bombers which had been standing by received orders not to take off. The result was that the "invaders" soon found themselves practically defenseless in the face of Russian MIGs, Stalin tanks and Czech machine guns.

What I had not known, however, was that the counter-revolutionaries inside Cuba, the fifth column, were a perfect model of disorganization and inexperience, and that the number of volunteers recruited in Miami for the operation was ridiculous; possibly Lenin was right when he spoke about "capitalist frivolity." Nor had I known that the four ships that carried the expeditionary force had been rented from a shipping company, that the majority of the officers on these ships were Spanish immigrants, among them some exiles, and that in Havana Fidel's Defense Committees had locked up two hundred thousand persons within a matter of hours.

All these additional bits of information, which were later repeated to me in New Orleans by the officers of said ships, were passed on to me by the Mexican, who was convinced that all this had strengthened Fidel's position immeasurably. "It's going to be very hard to organize any resistance movement in Cuba again," he said. "And as for outside Cuba, you see for yourself. Look at your pal the leader; there he is at the rail with a smile on his lips, watching Miami through his binoculars."

The "Guadalupe" continued her course southward. The heat increased. As soon as the Florida coast disappeared, the Cubans began buying all the cigarettes, cologne, and soap on board, much to the chagrin of those passengers who were going to stay aboard until Veracruz. The leader's wife, who had spent almost all her time playing solitaire, whispered something in her son's ear and the little future

Rebel Pioneer stood up and, without the slightest trace of shyness, began to sing:

> "Yes, now I have a motherland, I have a flag;
> Now I'm free and I'll have an education;
> What difference does it make if I lack a little,
> If I lack a little, if I lack a little soap?"

The hours that followed were devoted to the "maraca recital," to studying the maritime charts, and to asking the officers: "Where are we now, please? When are we going to arrive?"

We would probably reach Havana at dawn, but meanwhile we would have to put up with the frenzy of the Castro enthusiasts. At one point, an old fellow who had not left his transistor for a second managed to pick up the first Cuban station. "Viva Fidel!" he screamed, jumping up and down, "Viva Fidel!" Everyone flocked around him as a strong voice, much stronger than the young Rebel Pioneer's, blared forth from the machine's intestines: "This is Radio Havana, serving the Revolution." The flood of words swamped the ship. Fidel had learned his lesson well from Lenin and Hitler. The hammering away was persistent and continuous: "Fidel, Revolution, worms, Agrarian Reform, Soviet Union, imperialism, literacy campaign," and then all over again. "We need another hundred thousand Defense Committees!" "We must beat the Yankees in the spare parts battle!" "Cubans, the Revolution is waiting for you!"

The Cubans were weeping and I was overwhelmed by quite a different emotion, a terrible sadness. If only the minor mysticisms of our age could be channelled in a genuine, sincere, eternal direction; if only it were God Himself speaking over all the transistors on earth! The ship seemed insane, and the mulatto girl wandered about in vain looking for someone to attend her sleight-of-hand exhibition. The ship was a stratified little world, divided into control bridge, first-class and second-class passengers, and engine-room crew way down below in the bowels, many feet below the waterline; for this reason it did not capsize. But it was also a complex world and so there was no room for happiness, not even ploughing as we were through an ocean as lovely as the Caribbean.

After supper there was a movie, a German production. This time it was the German-born passenger who got excited. He saw his native land, the country where he had spent the Second World War in prison; his eyes, quite visible in the semi-darkness, were nailed to the screen. After the feature film a Walt Disney cartoon was shown, and it was like a breath of fresh air. Everyone had to laugh at the antics of the cat and the mouse, even the leader. He may have had Fidel's comment about the "treaty of the shark and the sardine" in the back of his mind but he laughed, along with his wife and son, and afterwards, when the lights had been turned back on, he came over to me and said: "You know, the 'Guadalupe' has treated us very well. We'll never forget it; even though you may not believe it, we're grateful."

4

---◆---

HAVANA

We entered Havana harbor after dawn. It seems that the harbor pilot's fee varies, depending on whether his services were requested for before or after sunrise.

The "Guadalupe" sailed past Morro Castle and anchored in the middle of the bay, an excellent position from which to observe everything. To our left, halfway up the hill, we saw the gigantic white statue of the Sacred Heart, whose head had been split by a bolt of lightning several months before. To our right, the Malecón, with its tall buildings and palm trees, much like any other seaside boulevard. On the sheds and warehouses of the wharves we could see signs reading: "Viva Fidel!" and anchored here and there in a relaxed, irregular way, the cargo vessels and oil tankers. I looked at these ships closely with my binoculars; almost all of them were from behind the Iron Curtain. Not a single crewman was to be seen. The ships looked deserted and hermetic, like every Soviet Embassy I had ever seen.

A few barges passed, carrying workers to the oil refineries and, farther in the distance, above the rooftops of the city, rose the ungraceful dome of the Capitol.

The shipboard Cubans, all done up in their Sunday best, had lined up along the starboard railing; the leader was at the head, with a flag wrapped around him. However, the ship was still quite a distance from the pier, where hardly a soul could be seen. What was going on? A lethargy hung over the entire port. At last, two motor launches pulled away from one of the piers and sped out to our ship. The Cubans were almost dancing with delight. "Viva Fidel! Cuba, sí; Yankees, no!" "Homeland or death!" The launches were full of militiamen and a few women. The militiamen were wearing the famous olive-green uniform and carrying machine guns. "Viva Cubaaaa . . ." they shouted; "Viva Fideeeel!"

I have seen few sights to match the enthusiasm of the moment when the launches came alongside the "Guadalupe." One of the militiamen shouted: "Welcome to the motherland!" "Death to the Yankees!" The passengers hollered back. Unfortunately, the ship's whistles blew just at that moment and the "Guadalupe" began to maneuver toward the wharf, obliging the launches to pull away to a more discreet distance. Conversation was impossible at that distance, so the militiamen and their lady friends decided to wave their berets in the air and sing a song I had read in the weekly paper *Vanidades*:

> "We're happy to be Socialists;
> We've just begun to live.
> Whoever doesn't like it,
> Can take a laxative!
> Cuchillo, cuchara,
> Long live Ché Guevara!"

The emigrants repeated until they were hoarse: "Whoever doesn't like it, can take a laxative! Cuchillo, cuchara, long live Ché Guevara!" But by this time the "Guadalupe" was almost ready to pull alongside the East Pier, which had been assigned to her, so that the launches had to withdraw, like it or not. It was then that the Cuban repatriates got their first big disappointment; the dock was practically deserted. Nobody was waiting to greet the "victims of the FBI's persecution." The port authorities had denied admission to even the families and close friends of the passengers, and as a result there was no one waiting at Customs except the mulatto dock hands, a few brick layers with chalky faces, and the impeccably dressed representatives of the Compañía Transatlántica in Havana. The Negro wrestler hadn't once stopped shouting "Viva Fidel!" and the whole Cuban party aboard joined in, but no one ashore replied. The porters, perhaps thinking back nostalgically to the golden age of tourism, to the days of the big transatlantic liners, were silent. The brick layers were silent too. Once in a while one of the militiamen on sentry duty lifted his arm in the air and shouted: "Long live the Revolution!", which was taken up by an ice-cream vendor and a man at the wheel of a yellow jeep with a big banner on the side saying: "Worms, to the firing squad."

As soon as the churning of the propellers had stopped and the gangplank was put ashore, the health, immigration and police officials came on board, along with the representatives of the steamship company, who brought me the current newspapers. "Cuban repatriates, please report to the Veranda Room with their passports," we heard over the public-address system. The Cubans looked at one another: Was all this bureaucratic red tape really necessary? "Please do not block the doorways." Little by little the

Cubans began filing in with their families and taking off their little flags and effigies of Fidel; they formed the classic line, with their documents in hand, and waited their turns. The leader pushed his way past in order to be the first one attended to. A bearded Cuban with him remarked in a familiar tone of voice: "The photographers will be here later on."

The police officials were two militiamen belonging to the G-2 Corps. They were obviously the masters of the port of Havana. With their veteran berets and big black mustaches they cut a rakish figure and wasted no time in heading for the first-class bar where, between sips of imperialist whiskey, they pompously informed the waiters that they put in volunteer duty every weekend cutting sugar cane, and that their children had been in the Escambray district for the past eight days, assisting in the literacy campaign. I decided to take some pictures of the scene going on in Immigration and went out on deck, but the intense tropical heat drove me back inside at once. It was as hot as Hades. The wharves, the wood, and the ship's canvas all seemed to be on fire and made breathing almost impossible.

I went into the Veranda Room and a militiaman immediately came up to me: "No photos permitted," he said courteously. I nodded and went to my stateroom to drop off my camera. In the meantime, the porters had come aboard and seemed to be in better humor. Some friends of the ship's officers had also come aboard and told us there was a monster rally scheduled in Havana for late that afternoon, featuring Rebel Pioneers and Young Rebels and presided over by Ché Guevara. Guevara was asking that the name "Patrice Lumumba" be given to a new industrial plant being built in Matanzas. They also told us that there were about a thousand Fidelistas with scores of signs and banners waiting outside the pier building to receive the returning Cubans. They had not been allowed to come on to the dock and were roasting in the sun. "I don't know what they'll do if this red tape takes very long," someone said.

The formalities were not going to be completed in a hurry, as anyone could see. The questioning was detailed and personal, which created a visible discontent among the immigrants. I took advantage of the delay to page through the papers given me by the Transatlantic Company's representatives. It was like listening to that radio again. The international news was supplied by Tass and the Chinese news agency Hsinhua. *Hoy,* run by Carlos Rafael, told of the arrival in Havana very soon of three hundred Russian agronomists. The reception program prepared for them was going to look like Queen Elizabeth's Coronation. *Combate* reported that, on its return voyage, the same ship that brought the Russian technicians would take a thousand Cuban children back to Russia for studies; the youngsters had been selected "from the best Revolutionary families." Another paper announced an anti-Franco meeting for that same night, in the Center founded years ago by Spanish immigrants from Galicia! Heading the roster would be "the Spanish General Enrique Lister," the Soviet Ambassador and "Colonel" Bayo, Fidel's guerrilla instructor in the mountains of Mexico. The treatment that this paper accorded Lister led me to suppose he had just arrived in Cuba and that his mission would be to supervise and check up on the orthodoxy of the revolutionary subversion movements in all of Spanish-speaking America. Throughout the rest of the papers there were revolutionary slogans mixed in with the ads. A good 50 percent of the movies being shown were from behind the Iron Curtain and a lot of attention was given to "Russian Cinerama." There were also ads for the Tropicana, Shanghai, and other night clubs and restaurants.

"Cuban repatriates may go ashore and proceed to the Customs office for luggage inspection and money exchange." A shiver of emotion swept the companionways and salons; Cuban soil at last! But what did that "luggage inspection" mean? Was the Mexican right after all? The Cubans, loaded with bundles, were bumping into one another in the corridors in their haste to get ashore. The first one to go down the gangplank was the leader, holding onto his son with one hand and the package of dollars he had collected in the other. Ashore the photographers, reporters, and others were waiting, along with a newsreel cameraman, who had climbed on the yellow Jeep. Once more it occurred to me that I might be able to get some good photos, but two bearded militiamen stationed near the ship's swimming pool made motions for me to stop.

The door of the Customs office was swallowing the "patriots" one after another. I left my observation point and went back into the first-class bar, where the two G-2 police were still drinking whiskey. I saw the passengers continuing to Veracruz asking for shore permits to visit Havana for a few hours, and I noticed the German with the combs unfolding a map of the city. All of a sudden a desire to go ashore came over me; would it be possible? I could disembark by myself without taking up the leader's offer. The temptation was tantalizing! I spent a quarter of an hour walking up and down the deck and saying "no" to a Negro on the dock selling maracas and bongo drums. Finally, I decided to ask for advice. "What could happen?"

The general opinion, very friendly and authoritative, was that "nothing could happen." My Spanish passport gave me the right to a transit visa. I could go ashore with no risks whatsoever, "so long as accompanied by the ship's officers, uniformed, and so long as I visited no one."

"The Cuban Government has orders to respect the officers of the Compañía Transatlántica, since it's the last line connecting Cuba with the United States."

"And why must I not visit anyone?" I asked.

"The Defense Committees are watching every house. Anyone who receives a visit from a foreigner is subject within half an hour to search, statement to the police, etc."

My wife and I looked at each other. Perhaps our fears were exaggerated. The ship's officers said they would be willing to go with us; they were all wearing their uniforms. A drunken voice floated up to us from somewhere on shore: "Worms, to the firing squad!" The temptation was tantalizing. . . .

My Mexican friend gave us the necessary push: "Go on and disembark; nothing will happen." No sooner said than done. We went to pick up our shore cards and change our clothes.

"Above all, don't buy anything ashore if you can't prove what money you bought it with when you return," we were told.

It was ten o'clock in the morning. We walked down the gangplank and into the Customs office, where we were confronted with the strange spectacle of the 250 Cubans being subjected to an intensive search; they were gathered together in little groups, whispering among themselves nervously. One woman came up to us and announced: "They're exchanging our dollars for Cuban pesos!" The fellow who had spent all day lounging around in his swimming trunks shrugged his shoulders and made gestures of amazement right in front of a militiaman, who snapped: "Something wrong, buddy?"

A policeman came over to us and said: "You may go through. Come this way, please." The officers preceded us out through the building. As we went out the door we saw the thousand Fidelistas we had been told about, roasting in the sun with their "Welcome" signs. Their reaction upon seeing us was completely unexpected. They greeted us with a deafening ovation, shouting at the tops of their voices: "Cuba, sí; Yankees, no!" They undoubtedly thought we were the vanguard of the Cuban repatriates or perhaps that we were the crew of some Soviet oil tanker. We made our way silently between two rows of the noisy reception committee. I never would have imagined that my arrival in Havana would be quite like this!

Once past the crowd, we were able to catch our breath. We found ourselves in a little square which reminded me of the ones in Cádiz. The asphalt was sizzling hot. The tinkling of a bell made us all look around: it was the ice-cream man with his cart.

Fidel's Havana! The first impression was staggering: rifles, more rifles, and machine-guns. There were rifles on every corner, guns on the balconies, in vacant lots, and on top of walls. Havana was an armed camp. The whole country was on guard duty—there were so many things to guard! The militiamen, many of them beardless, were on guard with their baggy pants. The militiawomen were on guard too, white, black, mulatto and in-between shades, wearing their hair long. Even the children were doing guard duty, one of them with a major's star. Maybe he had been Fidel's mascot in the Sierra or possibly he fought at Girón Beach when the "worms" landed.

Havana was, moreover, one immense propaganda poster. It was plain that Fidel was working through visual impregnation. We saw children's balloons representing Fidel and even the ice-cream cones bore little "Viva Fidel!" stickers.

We headed for the offices of the steamship company, where we found a long line of people waiting, especially religious and nuns, who wanted to leave the country. After that we went to the Malecón, the ocean drive. Some of the cars drove down the street emphatically, the ones carrying big-shots; other cars, belonging to the regime's nouveau riche, drove crazily; the taxis and private cars drove along with a certain shyness. Opposite, on the other side of the tunnel, we saw La Cabaña, the fortress turned into a prison. The sentinels walked up and down on top of the walls, or sat down with their legs hanging over the side. We were told that there were some 120,000 prisoners confined there, on starvation rations and subjected constantly to the hammering away of the loudspeakers and television. The word "television," Fidel's prime weapon, was brought up a hundred times that day.

We next headed for the commercial center of town. The steady din that the Cuban women aboard the ship had accustomed us to was now to be heard all around us on the street. We saw religious-goods stores open and intact, stands selling soft drinks and wonderfully aromatic coffee, street vendors selling Communist insignias and plastic articles, especially toys, grocery stores offering Chinese rice and Russian lobster and canned meat. Around the garages we saw big, impressive automobiles abandoned; they were American makes that needed some repair or other and, because of the shortage of spare parts, were now useless. We saw windows missing in many buildings; there was no glass to be had on the island, although they were waiting for a big shipment from Bohemia. Fats and greases were lacking, air conditioning was scarce and, above all, pharmaceutical products. This was apparently one of the worst problems Fidel had to face. The United States sent a little, but demanded payment in dollars. Negotiations were being held in Switzerland, but nothing had been settled yet. Meanwhile, in the hospitals, certain types of surgical operations could not be performed any longer because of the lack of anesthetics. In the maternity clinics the situation was critical, just as in the barracks, and even more so in the militia camps of one sex or the other, where venereal diseases were multiplying rapidly and hygiene was unknown.

Every hundred yards or so we ran into newsstands selling revolutionary periodicals and pamphlets with Lenin, Marx, or Stalin on the cover. We were shown the vacant lot, already cleared of debris, where the famous "El Encanto" department store had stood; it had been blown up by anti-Castro saboteurs some time before. Passers-by looked at us with curiosity and every so often some Rebel Pioneer waved to us or saluted us with a clenched fist raised to his temple.

We visited two book stores and it made my heart skip a beat to see how the propaganda reached up to the ceiling. There were hardly any copies of the Austral series of classics, and only a few novels, with movie-type dust jackets, printed in Mexico. The rest were all printed in Moscow, in Spanish, or put out by the Cuban Communist Party: *Anatomy of the Cuban Revolution, Fundamentals of the Socialist Revolution, The Dollar Empire, The Tragedy of American Diplomacy,* etc. There were Russian, Polish, Czech, and Yugoslav dictionaries and scientific manuals. There was little pornography, of course, in contrast to the

United States, where its abundance nauseated me. One of the book sellers told me that the police had rounded up all copies of *Doctor Zhivago* a short while before. I did see *Don Quixote* on some shelves. Dostoevski seemed to be taboo. There was poetry by Garcia Lorca; Machado was forgotten, as everywhere.

I was deeply impressed by the eager way some students and many adolescents paged through the books on display. I was just as interested in the textbooks and children's literature. Some Christmas books, in full color, had replaced Santa Claus with Lenin! Lenin appeared in Cuba from somewhere in Russia each year, giving Cuban children toys and promises of happiness and peace. As for the textbooks, the first letter of the alphabet taught was the "F," in order to be able to make sentences with the words "Fidel" and "fusil," the Spanish word for rifle. In the world-history books, the history taught was a history of the errors and crimes of capitalism and the Church.

I loaded up on all the most representative titles and the book sellers insisted on giving me a little hammer-and-sickle insignia. As we left the last book shop we ran into our friend the Mexican. He had brought his guitar ashore with him, and consequently the militiawomen who saw him took him for "a tourist joyously in favor of the Revolution," and began to sing to him: "Cuchillo, cuchara, long live Ché Guevara!" He informed the ship's officers that one of the Cuban repatriates who arrived on our ship had come up to him right on the street, begging him to try to get him back aboard the "Guadalupe." "You can't do anything to help him, can you?" he asked them. "I told him there was nothing I could do either."

Just as the Mexican finished his sentence, a sound truck drove past blaring the news that Kennedy was preparing a second invasion of Cuba. People on the street around us frowned as they heard this latest invention of Fidel. On the strength of this alleged second invasion he was maintaining a tense psychological climate and trying to justify the three hundred thousand-man militia; he had also undertaken the task of mining Havana from one end to the other, under the supervision of an engineer from East Germany. The Mexican told us: "Within a quarter of an hour, the entire city could be blown to bits. Everything would be reduced to rubble, like the 'El Encanto' department store."

We continued walking. The "Russian Cinerama" and "Socialist" films were advertized everywhere. We were told that the "Cinerama" was of a very high quality, as opposed to the other pictures which, according to unanimous opinion, suffered from the two big defects of Slavic motion pictures: slow pace and colossalism. It was a slowness quite alien to the Western mind and a childish, monotonous colossalism full of gigantic closeups which filled the screen.

I was especially anxious to visit the hotels and residential zones of Havana, occupied by the technicians from the East. On the way we saw churches open—the leader aboard ship was right—and convents closed, with various embassies turned into little islands full of political refugees seeking asylum. As for the hotels and tourist establishments, there were some practically empty even though Fidel insisted on maintaining an appearance of normality, with all the decoration and personnel just as before. Other hotels were filled to overflowing; their doormen and car hops had their hands full. There seemed to be a continuous stream of cars with exotic license plates pulling up in front or leaving, frequently with motorcycle escort. Apparently the Havana Libre, the Nacional and the Capri still air-conditioned their guests. As we passed, one of those spectacular "official" departures was taking place; inside a big black car we saw someone with an unmistakably Prussian head. The militiamen on duty presented arms, after a fashion, and the motorcycle policemen roared off in perfect formation.

"The technicians from the East!" My trip around Havana was very useful; it enabled me to pick up some first-hand information. In counter-revolutionary slang, these technicians were known as "Imperialists from the East." Many of them had never visited a factory in their lives, much less a sugar factory. They were mainly political agitators, especially well versed in every phase of revolutionary subversion. There were some of Spanish origin, who had been taken to Russia as children during the Spanish Civil War and subjected to intensive training. For some unknown reason, Ché Guevara was encouraging Cuban women to marry the Chinese, who were arriving in large numbers. Some funny tales were being told about these technicians. Some of them were amazed by their first contact with a series of Western delights that not even Fidel had been able to eliminate from the island, and they confessed more or less openly: "We can't understand why Cuba should be playing around with Communism." Others, upon their arrival, made up the most incredible questions about the magnificent sanitary installations, as though it were the first time they had ever seen such things. Some of them got roaring drunk. Still others left soon, complaining that the indolent Cuban character—the "Cuchillo, cuchara, long live Ché Guevara" song drove them crazy—made any systematic plan for socialization of the country impossible. All in all, the psychological shock was great, and the desired melding was never achieved.

Naturally, there were "real" technicians living in the hotels also, industrial engineers or agronomists for the most part, called in by the INRA. In general they were extremely efficient. Nevertheless, and quite apart from the language barrier—the Cubans who had worked in American companies were used to speaking English—in practice they turned out to be far more despotic than the Yankees. For every servant that an American had had, Cuba's "new friends" had two and, in addition, paid them less and demanded overtime, in the name of the Revolution and the proletariat. But the state surrounded them, above all the Russians and Chinese, with an almost mystical halo of redemption, and they were generally considered to be the Tropicana's and Shanghai's best customers.

All of a sudden, as we were walking along a street in the Vedado district, a pleasant Havana suburb, a bomb exploded somewhere. Instantly the G-2 Corps went into action, and the "Defense Committees" in every neighborhood were mobilized. Police jeeps and trucks roared through the streets, stopping passers-by. Our alarm was understandably considerable. One of the people accompanying us suggested that the best place to go to escape the dragnet was a restaurant called La Zaragozana, but that it was quite far away.

We decided to try it anyway, and apparently it was the white-uniformed officers with us who got us through without being stopped and questioned.

The restaurant looked inviting. Someone told us that Fidel himself ate there quite often: "He shows up at the most unexpected moments. Sometimes he asks for three helpings of something and then goes for two days without touching a mouthful. Usually he sits in the kitchen and drinks like a fish. He's the classic anti-methodical, anti-timetable, anti-everything."

We ate very well, especially seafood. Shellfish was plentiful as well as fruit and ice-cream. But we could feel everyone's eyes on us. The nearby tables were occupied by twenty-four-carat "revolutionaries" who were having a hard time maintaining their dignity, not to mention using their napkins and the proper fork for the fish.

After we had finished lunch, which we tried to stretch out to take advantage of the air conditioning, we went out into the street once more. We were approached by several lottery vendors—at the last moment Fidel had been obliged to preserve this and other "infamies" from the Batista days, under pressure from the many families that made their living by it—and we also saw several bearded militiamen pasting up a new poster which said: "Don't work for yourself, work for the Homeland." The text was much like the one on the posters plastered all over the airport passengers' terminal, for the instruction of visitors in transit: "Don't work for yourself, work for your country."

We would have liked to visit a church and several exhibits of "Socialist art," but at that hour, during the midday heat, everything was closed. We decided instead to drive out of Havana into the countryside. Our car simply headed out of the city without any particular destination, but we wound up driving in the direction of Santiago de las Vegas. The landscape was not especially pretty and moreover was pockmarked everywhere with sentinal posts, on hilltops and at crossroads. However, we did see a few palm trees with twisted trunks and some marvelous tropical plants called "flamboyants," whose red color is said by ancient legends to be due to the blood of the gods who died on the island.

The towns we went through were basically very poor. Up to now the Revolution has not changed their appearance, in spite of all the posters and promises. The sight of so many armed men and even little boys hanging around the corners and in the squares was anything but agreeable. Our car roared ahead right through the middle of these towns and as we passed were showered with cries of "Viva Fidel! Cuba, sí; Yankees, no!" Several times the militiamen mistook us for officers from some "friendly" ship, just as occurred in Havana, and came up to the windows to shake hands.

We saw any number of broken-down cars and even tractors in the ditches, and at every turn of the road saw signs saying: "Consolidated factory," "People's farm" or "This belongs to the Cuban people." Everything seemed to have been collectivized, "consolidated." The Ministry of Industry had also been at work, and not just the INRA.

Nevertheless, the number of successes had apparently been few. Industries considered basic, such as electricity, cement, metallurgy, synthetic fibers, etc. were closing down because of a shortage of raw materials and the equalized treatment shown to all the workers, which was quickly killing their initiative and incentive. The average worker was unhappy because he was also expected to do guard duty, sometimes at night, and even to donate blood for the hospitals. This last demand had met with special resistance, above all because many districts were left without medical care when so many doctors fled to Miami, and people had very little confidence in the militiawomen in white smocks. Outside one factory we saw a mobile medical unit; a steady stream of sullen men and women poured out, staring at the scrap of adhesive tape on their forearms.

As far as the agrarian reform was concerned, the situation appeared to be much worse. The worthless "bonds," the tariff that the Revolution imposed on everything, the sense of being tenant farmers to one big landlord, the state, had brought about a gradual confusion and exasperation which were not compensated for by the few areas of progress achieved, such as in milk production. The situation was critical, since in addition there was the drain of manpower for the militia, the havoc caused by the volunteer weekend sugar harvesting, due to the inexperience of some and the sabotage of others, and the steady exodus of young women from the countryside. All the young girls were strongly attracted by the so-called "People's Cultural Centers" in Havana. True, the agrarian reform and the "People's farms" had set up a few model plots, suitable for a visit by whichever Mikoyan happened to be in the country at the moment, but people who were familiar with rural Cuba could not hide their alarm—even Ché Guevara talked of it openly—especially in view of the fact that "agrarian Socialism" had always been a much bigger failure, in Russia and everywhere, than "industrial Socialism."

We passed many trucks full of men singing marches and patriotic songs. At one curve in the road we were suddenly confronted with an enormous bed sheet hung between two trees, with "Literacy Campaign" written on it. We stopped the car to get a better look. It was an improvised rural school, where one of the "literacy brigades" was at work.

The scene was frankly impressive. A group of young militiawomen—I wondered whether one of them, a particularly pretty young woman, might not be the famous Havana model, Norka—and Rebel Pioneers were teaching a group of old men from the local shanties to read and write. Each "literacy chief" was equipped with a blackboard, a big ABC book and a textbook. The pupils, divided into groups of six, were armed with a similar book, a notebook, a pencil, and a rubber eraser.

On the blackboard we saw: "Thank you, Fidel!", "Homeland or death," "We owe everything to you, Fidel!" Aside from their own signatures, these sentences were the first things the students learned to write. I recalled the "F" for "Fidel" and "fusil," and how Lenin had squeezed Santa Claus out of the Christmas books.

Our presence temporarily paralyzed the school. We found out that the majority of the old men were "fathers or grandfathers of heroes killed in the Sierra or at Girón Beach," and that some of the children came from remote districts. The militiawomen were sweethearts or sisters of other heroes and one could see a vision burning brightly in their eyes. One of them told me that she was going to be sent overseas soon, to Yugoslavia, on a "cultural" mission.

"The biggest problem with many of these old people is the fact that they have poor eyesight," she said. "That's why an oculist always comes the first day. It has been shown that before the Revolution 80 percent of our old people did not wear glasses or, if they did, had improperly ground ones."

The children seemed somewhat less unanimously happy. Some of them gave us the impression of being there under duress. Maybe they missed their families or perhaps their fathers were "counter-revolutionaries." Or possibly their "headmaster," a bearded militiaman well along in years, crammed them full of speeches or was too severe with them.

In spite of everything, the "Literacy Campaign" seemed to be one of Fidel's more fortunate brain children. Truly, there was something touching and lovely in that contact which joined such dissimilar generations in a common cause. The blackboards took on a redemptive significance. Fidel declared 1961 "Literacy Year" just as 1960 had been "Agrarian Reform Year." He wanted to ". . . eradicate illiteracy from the country in a hurry." Naturally, he would run into difficulties, as was to be expected. Coördination would slow down; desertions and weariness would take their toll. Maybe the whole thing would wind up being merely a romantic experiment under a palm-tree or beside the ocean. Nevertheless, that rural school, so austere, so poignant, so crazy, set up in the middle of the Cuban countryside, was like an oasis in a highway clogged with "consolidations" and guns.

We started out again with a warm send-off from the militiawomen and the bearded "headmaster," but we were soon to cut our little excursion short. Upon reaching Santiago de las Vegas we ran into such a mob of armed militia, with such cracked drunken voices—men and women alike were drinking straight out of yellow bottles and crowding around our car, shouting "Homeland or death!" and "We will win!"—that we became uneasy and turned around to head back to Havana by different roads.

From time to time we passed triumphal arches, which must have been erected to mark some model farm of the INRA and, here and there, signs advertizing some American product no longer for sale. Near a shabby little hut, ironically enough with its television antenna on the roof, we came upon a funeral procession. Four militiamen were carrying the coffin or a sort of stretcher, with the family and a dozen mourners behind. The little party's monotonous footsteps made the silent afternoon even sadder. Where was the cross, I wondered; where were the priest and the altar boys? The cross had been replaced by the

Revolutionary flag which covered the casket; the four militiamen were the priest, and the altar boys were off somewhere doing their bit in the literacy campaign. The funeral was consequently religious, in conformity with the new religion. The funeral consisted of a dead man and tears, like any other funeral; the only thing lacking was hope, that and God.

Without saying a word we continued on our way and re-entered Havana late that afternoon. The asphalt was still burning. As though of one mind and compelled by some higher force we all went into a chapel we saw open. It was an ordinary chapel, with two women praying in the half gloom. No one would have thought that outside newsboys would be hawking "New Cuba"; no one would have thought that at that moment an engineer from East Germany was laying mines from one end of the city to the other.

Shortly afterwards we had the monster rally to look forward to, the demonstration by the Rebel Youth and Pioneers that we had heard about on the ship. We were reminded of it by a roll of drums. We chose a strategic vantage point, so as not to miss a single detail, as the spectacle began to unfold before our eyes, presided over by Ché Guevara himself.

The number of boys marching in the parade toward the presidential palace was incalculable. The Pioneers were boys from seven to thirteen—I looked in vain for the young son of the "leader" from the ship—and the Young Rebels, armed with weapons, were boys from thirteen to seventeen. They were Fidel's two big hopes. I noticed that most of the boys were staring straight ahead with a clear and earnest gaze fixed on some far-off object. Again I thought of what the leader had told me: "By 1963 the new generation, the new Cuban youth, will be ready." Was he right?

And where did all that lead to? Fidel was racing ahead, telescoping all the progressive stages, advancing by leaps and bounds. In thirty months he had done more, in certain respects, than the Russians themselves in thirty years. We noticed that the Rebel Pioneers were shouting their petition that the Matanzas industrial plant be named after Patrice Lumumba, and moreover were asking for a "deal" with the United States: an exchange of the "worms," the prisoners captured in the invasion attempt, for tractors! This latter proposition hit where it really hurt. It had probably been dreamed up by Fidel himself; it is unlikely that Ché Guevara would have given the idea his approval. Guevara, who was only a few yards away from us at that point in the parade, was more cautious. He walked past with a very grave air about him, with a certain personal authority, not very far away from Father Guillermo Sardiñas, the famous priest who had been with Fidel in the Sierra and who wore a major's uniform in the parade.

The parade finaly passed, as the funeral procession had passed earlier, and with it we momentarily exhausted our collection of surprises. The evening papers came out with stories about a big American buildup at the Guantanamo base. The papers even had a photo of the "Guadalupe" with the repatriated "victims of the FBI" walking down the gangplank. I recognized several women in the photo. My mind was suddenly flooded with a whole world of memories, the entire passage from New York.

Our legs gave out at last, despite the frequent cups of coffee and the good lunch at La Zaragozana, so we decided to head back to the ship. The sunset bathed everything, even La Cabaña fortress, in a scarlet gold. We finally arrived at the docks, at the East Pier, where we were briefly and courteously questioned by the Customs men. As we walked on board, we noticed that the two G-2 men were still in the first-class bar, embracing one another fraternally and drinking.

After supper we finished off the day with television. There was a set on board and so we had a ringside seat for the "anti-Franco" rally being held at the Galicia Center as announced, with Enrique Lister as guest of honor. Lister! He had put on a great deal of weight since the Spanish Civil War, much more than Ché Guevara, who was at his side and looked much scrawnier than when we saw him marching with the Rebel Youth and Pioneers. To the left of the "Spanish general" we saw the Soviet Ambassador. There were ambassadors from Soviet satellite countries and, in a corner, with a rather simple expression on his face, we recognized "Colonel" Bayo, whom the announcer introduced as a "colonel" in the Spanish army and "commandant" of the Cuban army.

The meeting was a torrent of lies built around tiny grains of truth. One militiaman got up to say: "Fidel is a good man. He could just as easily kill the prisoners taken at Girón Beach but he doesn't, preferring instead to exchange them for tractors." Another militiaman read a list of statistics of artificial wood production, and then Ché Guevara spoke. He called Lister one of Cuba's dearest friends, to which the Soviet Ambassador agreed with a nod of his head.

Last of all, Lister himself spoke. He was the star attraction of the program, just as he had been in Spain at the battle of Belchite. He said that Cuba was giving an example to the whole world and was the vanguard of the proletarian forces which were preparing to liberate all Latin America from its imperialistic yoke of oppression. He went on to say that Cuba's heart bled to think of the suffering in

Franco's Spain and of the workers confined in prison. He declared that out of pity for the Spanish people it was important to abandon the idea of reconquering Spain through violence; it would have to be reconquered peacefully. "Nevertheless, if peaceful means are not enough, there will be no choice left except to resort to arms." And finally he greeted the Cuban people in the name of the Spanish Communists in exile, and announced that the Soviet Union was prepared to make any sacrifice necessary for world peace, a peace such as now reigned in Cuba thanks to Comrade Castro and the Revolution.

We switched off the set. What an unforgettable day! One fact stood out clearly: Fidel has left his mark, a dynamic and vital mark, on the Revolution. In some places it seemed to proceed at a donkey's pace, but in other sectors it soared like a helicopter. The most vivid characteristic of the Revolution was the unexpected. The Cuban people were advancing toward who-knows-where, riding on an unpredictable green flying carpet, between twisted palm-trees and "consolidated" business firms. Nobody knew what the government might decide that night or the next day. It might just as easily abolish the currency in circulation as decree that everyone on the island must study Chinese. One thing sure was that before long the last traces of individual freedom and private property would disappear from Cuba. Moreover, the radio was announcing that after July 26, the anniversary of the Olive-green Revolution, all exit visas would be cancelled.

5

FROM HAVANA TO SPAIN

We left Havana bound for Veracruz. In Veracruz there was a dock strike in progress, which prolonged our stop-over and made it possible for us to visit the Isle of Sacrifices, the city of Córdoba and the foot of impressive Mount Orizaba. The wife of our Mexican friend, the one with the guitar, was waiting for him on the pier and told us that the boarding of the Portuguese liner "Santa María," carried out by Galvao, and his men, was supposed to have coincided with the seizure of a Spanish ship in Veracruz. "It was intended to be a far-reaching chain reaction which failed because of lack of foresight." Later on, a Mexican policeman told us that the ship in question was the "Guadalupe."

From Veracruz we went on to New Orleans; to reach the port, we had to sail for nine hours up the great, oily Mississippi. It was one of the most memorable sights of the whole trip. We had a chance to speak in New Orleans with the officers of the ships that took part in the ill-fated "invasion" of Cuba on April 17, 1961; several of them were of Spanish origin. Their comments were unanimously of the opinion that, "it was the perfect occasion for confronting Russia with a fait accompli." "If the air support had not failed, the militia would have surrendered." They spoke painfully of the crew of the "Rio Escondido," the one ship sunk by Fidel's MIGs.

After New Orleans we made another call at Havana to pick up the priests and nuns who were returning to Spain after being expelled from Cuba, as well as several Cuban families who had managed to clear all the bureaucratic obstacles. On this second stopover in Havana I did not go ashore.

From the deck I watched the arrival of the new passengers. The Cuban families approached trembling; they were looking at the ground and ignored the insolent offer of the bongo drum and maraca seller to "take along a souvenir of Cuba." Even the children seemed aware of the fact that this was not an excursion but a drama. As these unhappy people came closer to the final check point, right at the foot of the ship, they could not conceal their panic and all the color drained from their cheeks. One could sense their relief, almost buoyancy, as they came up the gangplank. And finally, once safely on board, surrounded by discreetly understanding smiles of the rest of the passengers, they were overwhelmed by emotion and tears.

The priests and sisters appeared at intervals in the door of the Customs office. One by one or in pairs, they crossed the last section of dock with marvelous serenity, under the roasting sun. Their habits stood out as a challenge to many things. There were priests of all ages. They were travelling light, sometimes with only their passports in hand. One Christian Brother bought an ice-cream cone. A nun asked to be admitted to the ship's infirmary because she had a bad case of "Fidelitis." But the most moving scene of all took place as the aged Mother Superior of a convent of Sisters of Charity was ready to board the ship. She was ninety-six years old and had spent seventy of these years in Cuba taking care of orphans. Before climbing the gangplank she paused and knelt down, bending over as best she could, and kissed the ground. As she got to her feet she said: "I shall come back."

A total of 109 nuns and 21 priests of religious orders boarded. They were all Spanish with the exception of one nun of the Sacred Heart Order, who was Cuban. They were from many different types of orders: teaching, preaching, charity work. One missionary father had been expelled from four different countries in the past twenty years; one missionary sister, from three. The Dominicans' habit, a rough white, took on a special tint in the reflection from the blue sky and ocean. The mulatto porters called out names and cabin numbers, and shouted: "Coming through, please." The G-2 militiamen, with the rosaries around their necks dangling a hammer-and-sickle pin on the end, stared intently at the large crucifixes, devoid of gimmicks, that hung around the necks of the religious.

The "Guadalupe" began to maneuver away from the dock and toward the anchored oil tankers. We were going to say farewell to Cuba. All the passengers crowded to the railing. There were many pairs of binoculars in evidence, black binoculars "to bring things up closer." Unexpectedly, as we approached the center of the bay, several "friendly" motor launches darted out to us from the oil refineries, full of people who wanted to say good-bye to the expelled religious. "Sister Maria! Sister Dolores! Good-bye! God bless you!" The nuns, joyfully excited, recognized the voices and even the faces. "Good-bye, Good-bye!" On the Malecón too one could see little groups of people waving handkerchiefs, although closely patrolled by bands of militia in jeeps, and at one point there was someone on top of a truck, holding up a statue of Our Lady of Cobre.

The farewell was rudely broken up as one of the two launches that had met us when we first arrived sped toward our ship like a bullet and maneuvered in between us and the friendly boats. One nun, next to me, shouted at the bearded militiamen: "Savages, worse than savages!" But another sister, with whom I was later to have a long talk, murmured sadly: "May God forgive you all."

The militiamen maintained the position of their boat. They were following orders, just like the jeeps on the Malecón. They were trying to avoid another demonstration like the one the evening before, when more than four hundred religious sailed on the "Marqués de Comillas," also of the Compañía Transatlántica. The G-2 Corps had finally felt obliged to break up the throng congregated on the docks and did so with considerable violence.

Meanwhile, the "Guadalupe" was drawing nearer to the mouth of the bay, as an Italian ship was requesting permission to enter. The scenery was changing constantly, and some little girl's doll fell overboard and disappeared. In the sky, the atmosphere was becoming more rarified and an immense black cloud was forming over Havana. It was much like any other cloud, but it intensified the anguish of these people forced to leave Cuba against their will. The "Guadalupe" sailed on. The little groups of people on the Malecón were getting farther and farther away, scrawnier and scrawnier, as Ché Guevara had looked on TV.

At last we were in the open sea, bound for Spain. Havana lay behind us. For ten days the passengers of the "Guadalupe" would live together as a little community, isolated, surrounded by the Atlantic and by their own thoughts. The ship did not seem to be the same one that had carried us from New York. The change of passenger list had completely transformed it inside. A sweet, respectful silence crept into corridors and passageways formerly filled with tropical pandemonium. We soon noticed that the bars were empty but that, on the other hand, the chapel was always crowded. Instead of the leader, his wife and son, we saw the religious strolling on deck meditatively. The effigies of Fidel had disappeared, like the little girl's doll that had fallen into the sea. The nuns took turns praying the rosary. They prayed it anywhere at all, lined up on the benches or sitting on the covers of the hatches over the hold. On their heads, instead of pin curls, clips, and hair-nets, they wore white wimples, which led the ship's hairdresser to remark ironically that the trip was going to be a total loss for her. Several Spanish immigrants had come on at Veracruz, going back to spend their vacations in Spain. Among the Cuban refugees were an archaeologist and the former owner of a tobacco plantation. They were forever going out on deck, looking at the sea and remarking: "We're so glad." As they said it, they wept.

It was clear that the nuns were going to be the winged spirits of the trip. Among the 109 of them they formed a world as diverse as that of the crew. Some of them were quite ignorant and others were extremely intelligent and cultivated. There were some with experience and others who had still not lost their innocent, childlike gaze. A number of them knew nothing about seasickness pills and had never heard about artificial satellites or Mao Tse-tung.

Others, on the contrary, were quite up to date on world events. The superior of one convent had even read Lenin's pamphlet on revolutionary strategy entitled *Two Steps Forward and One Backward*. The most lovable one, without a doubt, was the old mother superior of ninety-six who had knelt down at the foot of the gangplank to kiss the soil of Cuba.

My contact with these nuns and priests was constant and fascinating. Their integrity inpressed me deeply; there were hardly any exceptions. The expulsion they had suffered did not bother them for their own sake, but rather for the sake of those they had to leave behind in Cuba. "Please try to understand," they told me. "We are eager to serve Christ anywhere, whether in the Caribbean or in Japan. But we feel so sorry for Cuba, for the sick and for the children who remain there. Who will take care of them? Did you see those little boats that came out to say goodbye? It almost broke our hearts."

Their reaction at finding themselves free was quite different from that of the Cuban families and the archaeologist and the tobacco planter. In reality, their faces—woefully pale from having been hidden away or unable to go out during the past few weeks—displayed something akin to deception. They were apostles, they had gone to Cuba to give everything. And they had come so close to doing just that! Perhaps that was it: they had almost tasted martyrdom. They had almost achieved it, but not quite. Physically, they were relieved but the sensation was ambivalent. Now they would have to go on living, they were sailing back to their native land, back to comfort and perhaps complacency, back possibly to routine.

My questions about their treatment met with a variety of replies, as was logical, since they were people whom Fidel tried to force into conformity, in spite of their individuality. Each church and convent suffered in a different way. "We were treated courteously. We were simply invited to put down in writing our loyalty to the Revolution. We refused and were expelled." "In our parish the militia entered with machine guns, destroyed the tabernacle, and accused us of hiding guns in the sacristy; we were arrested and finally expelled." "Six militiawomen showed up at our convent, convinced we were leading a soft life. When they found out we took care of the sick and how we lived, they almost begged us to stay." "They arrested me and beat me until I lost consciousness. Three times they pretended they were going to shoot me, but as you can see I'm still here."

All of this confirmed something already known: the religious persecution in Cuba did not have a homogeneous character, as it had had in Spain. It was by and large a bloodless persecution and consequently more subtle, except perhaps in Camagüey, where several priests had been brainwashed and nuns violated. In Camagüey, plays were given in the churches, the Young Pioneers were taught to shoot at the Holy Spirit and, at the time of the "worms' invasion," the militiawomen threatened to carry the nuns to the Sierra, "where the militiamen were short of women."

I asked when the systematic persecution of the Church had begun and how the Cuban people had reacted to it. Everyone agreed that at first, when Fidel came into power, after having fought in the Sierra under the patronage of Our Lady of Charity of Cobre, he tried to reconcile all the paradoxes in his little kingdom, so that the persecution did not begin in earnest until August of 1960. This was the month that the bishops published a joint letter in all the parishes, denouncing "the contacts of the Cuban government with the Soviet Union." Fidel called this document "counter-revolutionary incitement" and decided to take action. It was then that the insults began, the expulsion of the seminarians, who took refuge in Puerto Rico, etc. As for the reaction of the Cuban people, there were few encouraging signs. Cuba was considered the most indifferent nation in Latin America in religious matters. "Its chief characteristic is precisely that, indifference." "For this reason, perhaps, anti-clericalism hasn't been so severe as elsewhere, either." Even among the practicing minority there was a mixture of superstition, maybe of African Negro origin. Aside from this, there was the frivolous atmosphere of the island and a Protestant influence from the United States. In some villages there had never been a church. Entire regions could be considered mission territory. One eloquent statistic was the fact that out of a thousand priests on the island, only two hundred were Cubans.

One of my best sources of information was the nun who had asked to be treated for "Fidelitis" when she came aboard. She had once known Fidel's former wife. I asked her whether there had been many cases of apostasy among the nuns. "Among the Spaniards, none," she replied. "Among the Cuban sisters, two that I know of. They joined the literacy campaign."

The Spanish immigrants living in Mexico who had boarded in Vera Cruz frequently joked with the nuns. "Come to Mexico," they told them. "We'll treat you better than Fidel."

Little by little I came to notice that the archaeologist who was traveling with us, a tall, nearsighted and pessimistic man, was quite a scholar. As it turned out, he was to take the place of the Mexican in my friendship and confidence. In his opinion, there was another problem in Cuba just as grave as that of religion: that of the University, which was being turned into a Communist stronghold. Since this subject interested him very intimately, he spoke to me about it in detail. He felt that the blame fell squarely on Carlos Rafael, the "little Red billy goat," who insisted that, in view of the vacating of so many teaching posts, these positions should be given to competent professors "whatever their nationality." The idea, revolutionary and a bit absurd, opened the doors of the University to professors from the Soviet and satellite countries: Russians, Czechs, East Germans, etc. "Add to this the creation of 'School Cities' being built in the Sierra," said the archaeologist, "which will have a capacity of twenty-five thousand students and will become political experimentation camps."

It seemed to me that all this was quite in harmony with Fidel's unstable character. Since any number of the passengers on board had suffered imprisonment several times under Fidel, I became interested in the subject of repression, of the evolution that Fidel might have undergone in that area. Here too the opinions were unanimous. While he was in the Sierra, Fidel showed himself to be magnanimous with the soldiers and agents of Batista who fell into his hands. But once in power he changed completely. The number of deaths under his regime was perhaps exaggerated, but there was little doubt that it was high. The most repulsive aggressor of all was Raúl, Fidel's little brother Raúl, with his pigtail. "Raúl would have been a good henchman for Batista," everyone agreed. In any event, the one really responsible was Fidel himself since, apart from the public trials which had become world infamous, he had permitted so many abrupt executions without prior trial, the creation of repressive bodies like the G-2, and had opened concentration camps in Minas del Frío and Pino del Agua. "Fidel has become drunk with power and his own importance, and would be capable of any atrocity in order to stay on his pedestal."

I recalled the leader's words: "Why shouldn't someone inform on his brother if the brother is a counter-revolutionary?" I recalled the yellow jeep with the sign saying: "Worms, to the firing squad."

The whole thing was as clear as crystal. Fidel had crossed the line between the individual and the collective, and from there on anything went. Five deaths in La Cabaña were of no importance if they would help the Revolution. Besides, his intention was to spread the Revolution over the entire continent—wasn't that why Lister was there? Once that premise was established, a hundred deaths in Uruguay or Colombia meant nothing if they assisted the Revolution. It was the Soviet toboggan. A revolutionary had the right to seize an airplane in midair, to pirate a ship on the high seas, or, if the opportunity presented itself, to drop an atomic bomb on Washington, London, or Madrid without the slightest qualms of conscience. To begin with, the tobacco planter assured me, Fidel had printed thousands of copies of the pamphlet Bayo and Guevara had written on *Guerrilla Warfare* and was distributing them, along with arms, throughout all the mountains of Latin America.

The "Guadalupe" sailed full steam ahead, maintaining radio contact with the "Marqués de Comillas," the ship that sailed from Havana the night before. We found out that, besides the four hundred religious, she was carrying many Negroes who had declined the independence England had offered to the British West Indies and were going to Britain to work in the mines. Religious expelled from Cuba and Negro emigrants from the British West Indies—curious travelling companions, one of the many paradoxes produced at sea.

The Atlantic was kind that trip. Everyone went about his business. We put out a little daily paper which, thanks to everybody's co-operation, brightened the breakfast table. The rest of the day was spent in reading or playing games— I read the revolutionary books I'd bought in Havana— and swimming in the pool. At night there was usually a movie.

It seemed to me that the trip was bringing about a change in the distinct groups aboard the ship. The nuns were apparently forgetting that they had been deceived, that they had missed a possible martyrdom, and had reconciled themselves to the course events had taken. They lived their adventure with sweet resignation. They never complained, they took care of their sick, and they sang songs on deck, above all at sunset. When someone spotted a school of flying fish in the sea, there was a rush and flutter of starched wimples. They only spoke of Cuba once in a while. They offered Masses, Communions and ejaculations for the intention of the passenger who had underwritten the cost of all the telegrams they might want to send to Spain, noting that they had embarked without a cent. "We promise to use the least number of words. Thank you, sir." The more skillful set about embroidering a dozen handkerchiefs with the name of the ship's captain, don Alfredo Cuervas-Mons.

The Spanish emigrants who had boarded in Mexico were more or less the extroverts of the trip. They delighted in their well-earned pesos and invited everyone and his brother to have a drink, reminiscing about their unfortunate childhoods and their travel plans in Europe. One of them had brought along a color film of his daughter's wedding which he allowed to be shown one evening after the feature movie; it was like a quarter-hour breath of fresh air, with the whole ship enjoying the scenes of white veil and wedding cake. Alas, it was followed by an old newsreel which showed Fidel at the time of his trip to the United States. The Cubans in the audience forgot all about the white veil and the cake. One could hear a savage murmur sweep through the first-class bar, where the program was being held.

This was another of the changes I noticed being brought about during the trip: the Cuban exiles were thinking about Cuba now more than ever. Anything at all was liable to remind them of what they were leaving behind, so that their liberty was scarcely turning out to be joyful. I tried several times to bring up neutral topics of conversation, but without success. They were obsessed by the Revolution, regarding which they frequently expressed conflicting opinions. Some of them prophesied that Fidel's Babylon would collapse of its own accord: "Fidel has lost prestige." Others were sure that the United States would soon take a hand in the matter: "They'll have to do something soon." The archaeologist, always the pessimist, felt that it was a lost cause; not just the case of Cuba, but the whole struggle between capitalism and Communism. Just like the leader, he felt we were witnessing the beginning of the end of a civilization. Basing his opinions on his extensive historical studies, he cited cases of the disappearance of remote cultural groups to prove his point. The tobacco planter, on the other hand, quite refused to give up so easily. "I want to regain my land, and I shall," he said.

Of all the Cubans, one stood out in particular, a young fellow, short and thick-lipped. He made fun of the others because they were intent on getting to Miami, and planned to remain in Spain just long enough to put their papers in order at the American Consulate. He was planning to do no such thing. He was disillusioned and had made a picturesque decision: he was going to Andorra and ask the authorities to grant him Andorran citizenship.

He justified his decision, a philosophical one, by displaying a scar on his throat, received while fighting Batista, and another on his forehead, a souvenir of his resistance to Fidel. "I'm equally disgusted with Khrushchev, Miró Cardona and the Wall Street bankers," he confessed. He had turned into a political sceptic and wanted to make his home symbolically in some insignificant, neutral country; he had decided on Andorra. He never even wanted to see the ocean again, since he felt that people in the mountains or the interior were more noble and loyal than islanders. In Andorra he would live in peace.

The traditional Captain's Ball was a real pleasure for the Cubans; it was a wonderful party, and the night was as lovely and gentle as a blue Andorran one. The Cubans dressed up, drank champagne and danced to the music of the ship's orchestra. They wore all sorts of big cardboard noses, funny hats, eyeglasses with no glass in them, and other disguises, but nobody wore a false beard. Their laughter gradually dissolved the terrible complexity of emotions they had experienced since first coming aboard and they finally managed to relax and enjoy themselves. The archaeologist won first prize in a balancing contest that consisted in walking a straight line with a pile of books on one's head. The tobacco planter crawled in and out among the legs of the tables like a cat, much more agilely than anyone else. Somebody was playing every minute of the time that evening, even if it was only the drums. At last, about four in the morning, with a shout of: "Cuba sí, Russia, no!", the last of them straggled off to their cabins, lulled by the monotonous hum of the engines, rising from some intestinal world sunk several meters below the water-line.

A memorable event for most of the passengers was the impromptu sermon given by the young priest who had almost been executed three different times. He was a man endowed with a poetic nature, and celebrated his nameday by talking to us of Jesus and the sea. One by one he mentioned the Gospel texts referring to Jesus' contacts with the sea, giving special emphasis to the time when He calmed the waves and the other time when He walked upon the waters. At the end he alluded very soberly to the persecution in Cuba, recalling Jesus' words to His Apostles: "When they persecute you in one city, leave and flee to another."

We all followed closely the march of the little flag-pins across the nautical map, representing our ship's course. We had already overtaken and passed the "Marqués de Comillas." The weather was fine and the little flag-pins told us that La Coruña, Spain, was near, but it was hard to bring oneself to believe the fact . . . the ocean was so enormous! Not one ship passed; not a single plane flew overhead, not even a bird. The radio operator was our only link with land, except for an occasional Portuguese or Spanish radio station that one of the stewards would manage to pick up on his transistor.

These stations unknowingly demonstrated to what degree geography determines peace or anxiety. The slogans that so stirred up Fidel's militia in Havana or Camagüey had no meaning whatsoever in Lisbon or La Coruña. Man had not yet succeeded in rising above the tribal stage; we still lived in little airtight capsules, like Yuri Gagarin in his globe-circling flight. We cultivated, even in the intellectual sphere, tiny independent parcels of land that no INRA on earth could consolidate, and we did not even select for ourselves the seed to be sown there.

This was one of the subjects developed by the ninety-six year old nun, such an expert in matters of loneliness—seventy-two years taking care of orphans. She maintained that Cuba had become a Communist capsule, whose marrow was in Moscow, and that in the center of this capsule were known the present and future of the country. She was not a pessimist like the archaeologist—she had promised: "I shall come back"—but neither did she believe that Fidel had lost all of his prestige. She judged that the Cuban ruler could still draw a crowd of a million in a public square anytime he felt like it, and that it would be a mistake to imagine that eight hundred thousand would attend under compulsion. The masses were as ignorant as an orphan and instinctively needed a Redeemer, so that it would take a hundred Raúls and a hundred Listers and a good many years to bring them to their senses. They did not reason in the same way that people reasoned in La Cabaña, or in a counter-revolutionary get-together, or in the bars aboard the "Guadalupe." Fidel could still count on strong support and was clever enough to keep on pulling cards out of his sleeve to continue fanning the sacred fire. "The Cuban people would turn on him only out of hunger, and hunger —a hunger for truth—will be a long time in reaching the island.

The little flag-pins put an end to all this one morning when we suddenly spotted the fog-shrouded coast of Galicia, much more abrupt than that of Florida. The Compañía Transatlántica, the only passenger line still serving Havana, had carried us safely back to Europe, to Spain. Everyone hurried up on deck and once again the binoculars were brought out. The memory of our departure from Havana, of the black cloud over the Capitol, of the oil tankers with invisible crews, of the statue of Our Lady of Charity, patroness of Cuba, held aloft from the roof of a truck on the Malecón—all these memories rushed through my mind, and perhaps the mind of more than one of the other people on board.

Standing on the bridge, beside the ship's friendly officers, I felt overwhelmed by a tremendous sadness. Europe! What an emotion-packed word, the only word that came to my mind. I had seen so much since that morning of April 9 when we left Bilbao aboard the "Covadonga." I had seen a little slice of America, enough to get an idea of the incredible distance between New York and San Francisco, between Veracruz and Mexico City. Near Philadelphia I had seen an airplane graveyard and near Santiago de las Vegas I had seen a dreary funeral, devoid of hope. I had several points of reference: a young woman had called me an "imperialist" in a voice filled with hatred, a stranger of German origin had given me a comb, and I had met a young man who wanted to move to little Andorra. The mottos "Homeland or Death!" and "We shall win!" became mixed in my mind with the songs of the nuns at dusk and with the leader's words: "Even though you may not believe it, we're grateful." I thought of Kennedy, his youth, his promises: "We shall never abandon Cuba." I thought of the first, impudent question Stevenson had asked me in the Waldorf Astoria: "And which side did you fight on in the Spanish Civil War?" Yes, the only word that came to my mind was "Europe," a Europe united from Scandinavia to Gibraltar. Would England enter the Common Market? The "Marqués de Comillas" was carrying four hundred Negroes to work in her mines. Would De Gaulle continue to bleed France? In Lisbon I had seen a thousand Portuguese soldiers leave for Angola; a thousand, that was the exact number of Cuban children who must have been sailing to Russia right at that moment. Europe was the only possible hope for liberating Cuba, in an indirect way, through pressure; the exiles in Miami would never do it. Ché Guevara would continue marching near Father Sardiñas for a long time to come unless Europe formed a compact and authoritative block, the Third Force, an intrusive force, at once centrifugal and adhesive, between the White House, the Kremlin and Mao Tse-tung's palace. Europe would have to declare the coming years "Literacy Years" and teach the East and the West that the only proper common meeting ground for man's understanding with man was a happy blending of historical experience, religious sentiment, and scientific experiments yet to come, like that performed in Bologna. To bend intellectually and spiritually before Russia or China, before the United States or Cuba, would be suicide. It was a crucial moment. Russia and the United States might reach the moon, China might reach the peak of demagogy, but Europe had to reach the Earth. She had to reach the Earth as soon as possible, because she had known it for centuries, had beautified it and made it prosper.

Unfortunately, over the coast of Galicia, over Europe, a dense fog was forming. From the bridge of the "Guadalupe" it was hard to tell whether any one shape was a rock, a piling, or a tired man. And no matter how much the ship's whistle called, the harbor pilot, the guide, was slow in arriving.